Compendium of Celtic Crafts

SEARCH PRESS

Compendium of
Celtic Crafts

Judy Balchin, Courtney Davis,
Vivien Lunniss and Suzen Millodot

First published in Great Britain 2008

Search Press Limited
Wellwood, North Farm Road,
Tunbridge Wells, Kent TN2 3DR

Reprinted 2009 (third), 2010

Chapters 1 to 4 are based on the following books published by Search Press:

Celtic Illumination by Courtney Davis (2001)
Celtic Calligraphy by Vivien Lunniss (1999)
Celtic Knots for Beaded Jewellery by Suzen Millodot (2006)
Celtic Glass Painting by Judy Balchin (2000)
Classic Glass Painting by Judy Balchin (1999)

The projects in Chapter 5 are by Judy Balchin and are based on those published in *The Complete Book of Celtic Designs* (2008).

Text copyright © Judy Balchin, Courtney Davis, Vivien Lunniss and Suzen Millodot, 2008

Photographs by Charlotte de la Bédoyère, Search Press Studios; and Debbie Patterson, Search Press Studios

Photographs and design copyright © Search Press Ltd. 2008

ISBN: 978-1-84448-355-6

Suppliers
If you have difficulty in obtaining any of the materials and equipment mentioned in this book, then please visit the Search Press website for details of suppliers: www.searchpress.com for a current list of stockists, including firms who operate a mail order service.

Publishers' note

All the step-by-step photographs in this book feature the authors demonstrating art and craft techniques. No models have been used.

Printed in Malaysia

Acknowledgements
The authors and Publishers would like to thank John Wright of Pebeo UK Ltd., Unit 109, Solent Business Centre, Millbrook, Southampton, SO15 OHW for supplying the glass paints; Edding UK Ltd., Merlin Centre, Acrewood Way, St Albans, Herts, AL4 0JY for supplying the Marabu Fun & Fancy peel-off paint; David Rabone of Regalead Ltd., Sharston Road, Manchester, M22 4TH for providing the self-adhesive lead; Philip and Tacey Ltd., North Way, Walworth Industrial Estate, Andover, SP10 5BA for supplying the Dutch metal leaf; Black Dragon Crafts in Wales for supplying the Celtix beads and pendants used in many of the projects in Chapter 3; and John Winstanley of Blot's Pen and Ink Supplies, 14 Lyndhurst Avenue, Prestwich, Manchester for his help with the materials in Chapter 2.

Page 1
The early Christian Celts would not have used the heart shape, which is a much more recent symbol, but the interlaced pattern is typical of Celtic design (see page 120–121).

Page 2
Celtic chalice (see page 138).

Page 3
Celtic knotwork combined with beads decorated with Celtic designs are combined to create this stunning necklace (see Chapter 3).

Page 4
A traditional Celtic knotwork design (see page 14).

Page 5
A traditional Celtic spiral design (see page 159).

ontents

Preface

The Celtic civilisation has exerted a more lasting influence than almost any other. It flourished in Europe before the Roman Empire and Christianity, lasting for over a thousand years from the sixth century BC to the ninth century AD. Today, Celtic languages are still spoken in Brittany, Ireland and parts of the British Isles, and the Celts' beautiful, stylistic and intricate designs are as popular as ever.

Early Celts lived a pagan life, as farmers, warriors and artists, worshipping natural forms such as Mother Earth, the stars, the sun and the moon. Because of their oral tradition, they had no written records, but would memorise events, incorporating them into chants and prose. These were recited by bards, who entertained and educated the tribes. They in turn passed the mythology on from generation to generation. During this early period, artists worked in stone and metal, using their skills to create monuments, weapons and jewellery.

It was not until the fifth and sixth centuries AD that British and Irish monasteries were established and workshops set up to produce illuminated manuscripts and books. These now provide us with a wealth of Celtic artistry. A page might feature only one word, perhaps a capital letter, but this is infused with life – decorative motifs mixed with interlaced creatures, stylised figures, angels – and ornamentation purely from the artist's imagination.

This compendium brings together the work of various artists and craftworkers who have drawn inspiration from Celtic art and design. It begins with a basic grounding in Celtic illumination – the symbols that typify Celtic art. This is followed by a chapter on Celtic calligraphy, showing you how to create the beautiful letterforms used by the seventh century scribes. In Chapters 3, 4 and 5, traditional Celtic designs are placed in more contemporary settings, providing ideas and inspiration for a broad range of jewellery, painted glass objects and paper crafts. No previous experience in any of these crafts is needed as full instructions are given.

It is hoped this book will prove a useful reference and source of ideas for anyone interested in the art of the Celts. Draw on their energies, be open and receptive to their influence and guidance, and your creativity will flourish!

A Celtic cross from a churchyard in St Fagans, Wales. A wonderful example of the combination of exuberance and control in Celtic knotwork.

Celtic Illumination

The symbols which typify Celtic art had been used by different cultures for thousands of years before adaptation by the Celtic people. The imagination and skill of the Celtic craftsmen took these symbols further, embellishing and creating even more detailed and complex forms. Illuminated works such as the books of Kells and Durrow were the culmination of a long history of art.

The knotwork pattern is the most recognised form of the art, though it did not appear until late in Celtic history, and was used in its pure form for only a relatively short period. Celtic knotwork symbolises infinity and the continuity of the spirit in this world and the next.

The circle or disc is considered to have been man's first step into art. It was seen in nature, in the construction of animals, birds and insects. It also symbolises the sun and moon, male and female, heaven and earth. From the circle came the spiral, symbolising growth. The direction of its motion represented either positive (clockwise) or negative (counter-clockwise) attributes. Early Celts used the spiral to ornament scabbards, shields and other metalwork.

Key patterns have a long history and examples survive from as far back as 20,000 to 15,000 years BC. They evolved from spirals constructed with straight lines rather than curves. When connected, they formed complex labyrinths. Both key patterns and spirals are associated with protection and were often used to protect warriors, their weapons, homes and final resting places.

Zoomorphic ornament is based on the forms of animals, birds and reptiles. Its origins are the worship of animals and their power, and the earliest images are found in caves. It appears early in Celtic art but reached its height much later, as elaborate carvings on Pictish stone slabs and in illuminated books. Animals like the boar or stag

represented the spirit of the forest and hunting, as well as prosperity and fertility. It was believed that the serpent – symbolising resurrection – regained its youth by shedding its skin.

This chapter provides simple ways of creating knotwork, spiral, key and zoomorphic patterns. For those of you who are not mathematically-minded, the use of tracing paper and light boxes makes planning the work a little easier, though it still takes time and the right frame of mind. One tip is to make a template which can be flipped or duplicated, yet will link effectively with the next panel. At first the patterns may seem frustrating, but as with physical exercise, you must break through pain barriers. Once you reach the other side, the rewards are tremendous.

Materials and Equipment

These are the wands, potions and other ingredients with which to create your magic. Always keep your tools clean; there is nothing more annoying than marking the border of a picture with a dirty ruler or inky fingers.

Paper

2-ply heavyweight paper is ideal for finished work, as the surface gives a clean, even pen line. Work in a larger size than required so that when the image is reduced the lines look smoother and the image sharper.

Tracing paper

Use to build up layers of doodles, which can be transferred to the light box. Join tracings with adhesive tape when planning a design.

Pencils

Use a soft pencil – a 2B is ideal – for doodling, tracing, and working out rough designs.

Eraser

Use a soft eraser to rub out any unwanted lines or adjust a design as you plan it.

Paints

All the images in this book have been created using gouache: permanent white plus just eight colours – Bengal rose; flame red; brilliant green; spectrum yellow; marigold yellow; ultramarine; cerulean blue and sky blue. Remember these are the magic ingredients of your picture, so keep the water clean.

Palette

Use this for mixing colours.

Pot or jam jar

For holding water.

Brushes

It is hard to believe the illuminators of the past created such intricate work with the simple tools to hand. Thankfully we do not have to make our own brushes and can choose from a vast range. To achieve the fine strokes necessary for detailed work, natural hair brushes are preferable, but less expensive alternatives are available.

Toothbrush

An old toothbrush is ideal for flicking paint over areas of your design to create different effects.

Technical pens

Ink pens have developed over the years, and you no longer have to spend ages unblocking the nib only to end up covered in ink as you try to refill it. Easy, clean cartridges which slot into place save a lot of time. Use either a 0.35 or 0.25 size according to the detail you are adding.

Protractor and set square

Use the protractor to divide your design into accurate segments, and the set square for right angles.

Ruler

You will need this for measuring and for drawing straight lines.

Compasses

You will need compasses to draw circles and arcs in your design, preferably with an attachment for holding pens and refillable pencils.

Masking tape

Useful for fixing your design to a light box or working surface.

Self-adhesive memo notes

Use to protect the edges of your design, or to frame areas which are to be speckled. The low-tack adhesive will not pull paint from the surface of your work.

Talcum powder

Before working on an image put a little talcum powder on a cloth and wipe over the paper to remove any grease on the surface.

The light box

Though not absolutely essential, a light box will make such a difference to your work, you will wonder how you managed without one.

In the photograph below, a larger sheet of glass has been laid over the light box to provide a bigger working surface. If you do this, make sure both the light box and glass are firmly secured before beginning.

You may find it easier to fix your work to a loose sheet of plastic rather than to the glass of the light box. The point of compasses will 'bite' into plastic to give a good hold when you are drawing circles or segments, but it is bound to slip on glass no matter how thick the paper used. The plastic can be rotated to provide the most comfortable position as you complete different sections; you will not be able to achieve an even line if your body is at an awkward angle. Secure your drawing to the plastic sheet with adhesive tape, double-sided tape or pliable adhesive. If you have more than one plastic sheet, you can use it to work on roughed-out sections of your current picture. Extra sheets are also useful if you want to work on several projects at once.

Working with Colour

Colour is one of the most universal of all types of symbolism. The intensity of colour and its purity correspond to the purity of symbolic meaning; primary colours correspond to primary emotions, while mixed colours express a more complex symbology.

Blue in Jungian psychology is associated with the clear sky and stands for thinking, and the Virgin Mary's robe is usually depicted in blue, probably because of her status as queen of heaven. Yellow and gold represent the sun, intuition and illumination; red represents blood and emotion; orange, fire and purification. Green is a soothing, restful colour symbolising nature, growth and fertility, and predominates in Christian art because it is a bridge between yellow and blue. Purple – a mixture of the fire of red and the calm and thoughtfulness of blue – represents power and sublimation and is the colour of the Cardinal's robe.

Before working on your picture, make some photocopies of it and try to let the colours choose themselves. If the result is a mess, fine – it is only a photocopy. With perseverance and by letting instinct and inspiration rather than will guide your brush, you will begin to tap into another level of satisfaction with your endeavours.

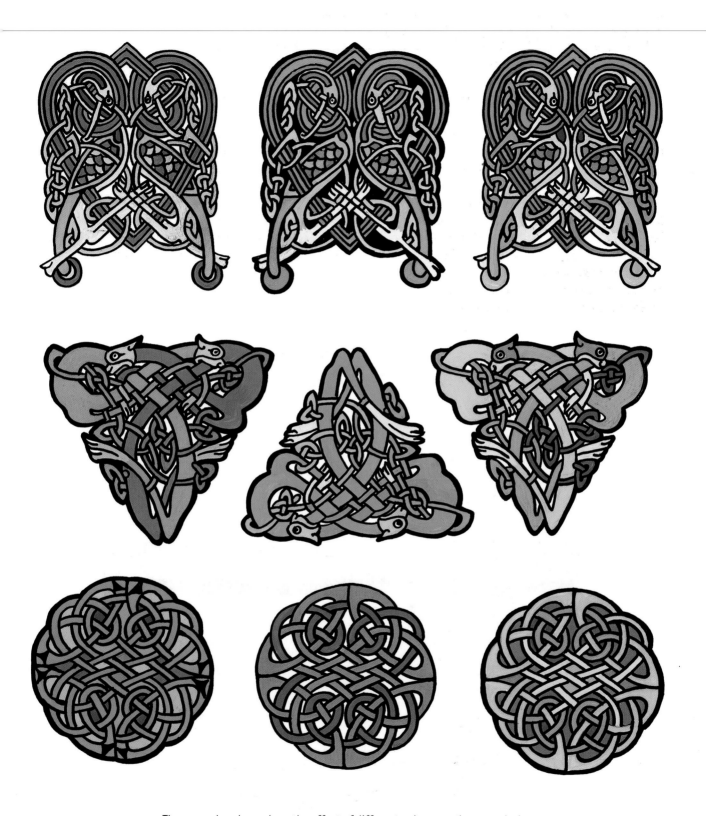

The examples above show the effect of different colours on the same design.

Knotwork

The very sound of the word 'knot' conjures up an image of difficulty and problems, though there is also the more positive image of tying the knot, and uniting two souls in marriage.

At first glance, knotwork patterns can be overwhelming in their intricacy, but it needn't be so. If you never look under the bonnet of your car because you are terrified that you may cause more problems than your non-mechanical brain can deal with, then remember it is just fear of the unknown, and that a few lessons in basic car mechanics will

work wonders. You may never aspire to the mystical reaches of the broken 'big end' but when things are explained simply, you will at least be able to fill the screen washer. So it is with Celtic artwork, and as you work through these pages the mechanics will become clearer.

Remember the feeling of relief when you manage to undo a spectacularly difficult knot; that sense of achievement over adversity – and perhaps even the discovery of a few brief moments of stillness as a reward.

We speak of the rich tapestry of life. The Cosmic Pattern, above, draws on the symbolism of the Celtic knot, capturing the idea of the continuation of life, death and rebirth in an endless knot with no beginning or end.

The sacred thread

Simple plaitwork designs can be traced to ancient Greece and to artefacts from prehistoric Mesopotamia. Thousands of years before Celtic artists adapted these patterns they were powerful symbols, used daily as spiritual tools to help with hunting for food and in the veneration of the Creator. Shetland fishermen believed they could control the winds by the magical use of knots. A knotted cord forms a ring which signifies both an enclosure and a protection. The silver cord in Vedic teaching is the connection between the physical body and the astral body, broken at the point of death so the spirit can journey into the next world. A continuous thread twisted into a figure of eight emphasises the relationship of the knot with infinity, and is its most popular significance in Celtic art today.

Although knotwork is widely regarded as the main Celtic pattern form, it came into use after spirals, zoomorphic, key and step patterns. It was useful for filling in broad and difficult areas on stone and vellum. Craftsmen who experimented with the monotonous plaitwork found that by breaking the bands, they could introduce new patterns of complex knots and widen the scope for secondary designs.

This panel shows how a uniform knotwork design can be broken into, creating patterns within patterns.

In 1904, J Romilly Allen, an early specialist in the field of Celtic art, identified eight basic knots which he believed to be the basis of most Celtic knotwork.

*The patterns above give you some idea of the many variations
which can be achieved with single and multiple threads.*

Designing knotwork

The following steps are a guide to your first knotwork design. For simplicity, these show a pattern in four segments, but as you gain confidence, your design can be divided into any number of segments.

Achieving this is easy: for a circular design all you need to know is that there are 360 degrees in a circle. Divide 360 by the number of segments you want in your design to find the number of degrees per segment, then use a protractor to mark these out around the circumference of the circle. Complete as shown.

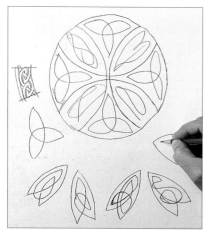

1. Start doodling design ideas with a soft pencil, incorporating ideas for individual segments.

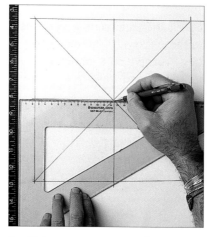

2. Using a set square and beginning with a right angle, draw up a grid on tracing paper.

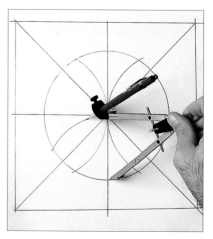

3. Draw the inner circle of the design with compasses using the grid as a guide. Draw segments.

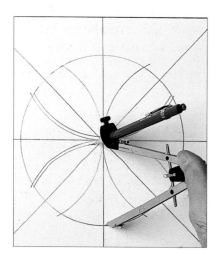

4. Reduce the span of the compasses. Draw a second segment inside each of the first segments.

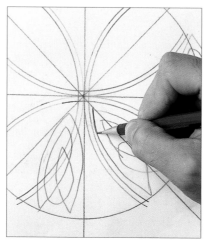

5. Place your chosen rough sketch under tracing paper and trace in one of the segmented areas.

6. Remove the rough sketch from the first segment and complete the details freehand.

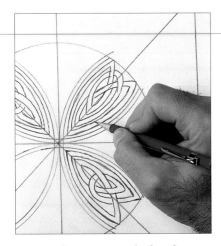

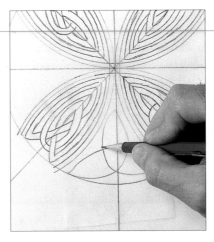

7. Use the same rough sketch to complete the opposite segment. Select a different rough sketch for the two remaining segments.

8. Fill in the remaining segments in the same way, first tracing the designs and then completing them freehand.

9. The finished rough design, which will be the inner circle of your completed pattern.

11. Insert a design into the first section of the outer border. This will be repeated sixteen times.

10. Draw a second circle outside the first. Add two more circles which will enclose the outer border.

12. The completed rough design for inner circle and border.

13. Transfer the rough design to the light box. With a technical pen, mark the outlines carefully, neatening any lines and refining areas.

14. Begin to fill in the design, using a No. 2 brush. Here Bengal rose has been used with a dash of white, then Bengal rose blended with yellow.

15. Build up the design using colours of your choice.

16. Complete the inner circle and begin work on the outer border of your design.

The completed knotwork design.

*Knotwork designs can be adapted to any shape, and careful choice
of colours can complement the intricacies of the pattern. The
example above is from the Book of Durrow.*

Knotwork borders

The idea of creating a knotwork border that will join up neatly can be daunting, but with some tracing paper or a light box, photocopier or scanner anything is possible. Using either tracing paper or a light box, create a rough of your proposed border – which can be square, oblong or round – then quarter it up. Decide which knotwork panel you intend to use, to determine the thickness of the band of the border. Instead of trying to design the whole border at once, the steps opposite begin by working on one section at a time, inserting one section of border before moving on to the next.

Tip

Simple knotwork patterns are very useful to end or link one or more spiral bands.

You might like to choose from this selection of knotwork panels, copying, enlarging or reducing to fit.

Square border

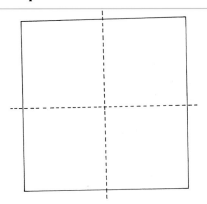  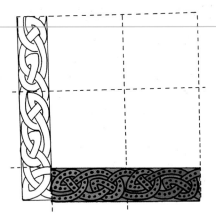

1. Draw a square and divide it into four equal sections.

2. Choose the border you wish to use. You may find it easier to choose from the selection left.

3. Mark out the border area and quarter the square left inside. This gives the width of each section and leaves a box in the corner.

Circular border

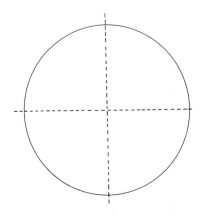  

1. Draw a circle using compasses and divide it into four segments.

2. Choose the border you wish to use, noting that each section will have to be adapted to fit the curve of the circle.

3. Mark out the border around the edge. Divide the segment to produce the individual panels.

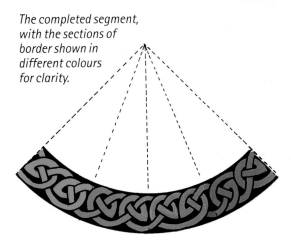

The completed segment, with the sections of border shown in different colours for clarity.

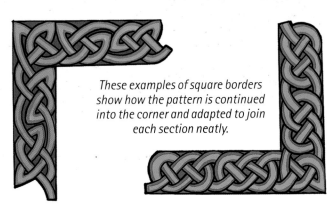

These examples of square borders show how the pattern is continued into the corner and adapted to join each section neatly.

*Knotwork designs may seem complicated, but will
become easier with practice – why not try a square
or rectangular variation?*

*This selection of knotwork borders may
help you to gain the confidence to begin
designing your own.*

Spirals

The spiral was the earliest decorative motif used in Christian Celtic art, but with the corruption of Celtic illumination it was also the first to disappear around the tenth century AD. Its symbolic centre is that of the Most High God round which all things revolve, the spirals stretching from the centre emphasising this movement.

With the circle, the spiral is probably one of the oldest patterns used by man. It is seen time and again in nature, and in art the whorls have been used to represent the evolution of the universe and the growth of nature. It features in primitive dance rituals for healing and initiation ceremonies, symbolising escape from the material world and entry into the Otherworld through the 'hole' represented by the mystic still centre.

Although spiral ornamentation appears complicated, you can gain a great deal of satisfaction from winding and unwinding the coils from one to the next.

A spiral modified from a design in the Book of Durrow.

A sense of balance

Many spiral patterns achieve a sense of balance by contrasting clockwise (positive) and anti-clockwise (negative) spirals. In Neolithic times, the spiral seems to have been an essential barrier to the inner sanctuary of a stone burial chamber, like the stone at the entrance to the tomb at Newgrange in Ireland (below). The passage beyond the entrance stone symbolised the soul's journey from death to rebirth at the still centre. The inner chamber of the tomb was used for both meditation and initiation, and the early Celtic saints continued this tradition by using rock cavities and beehive stone huts for meditation and prayer.

Tip
The patterns on the facing page have been broken down to show the method of construction.

Spiral patterns decorate the chambered cairn at Newgrange, Ireland, which dates from 3200 BC.

Bronze scabbard blade engraved with spiral designs; Ireland 300–400 BC.

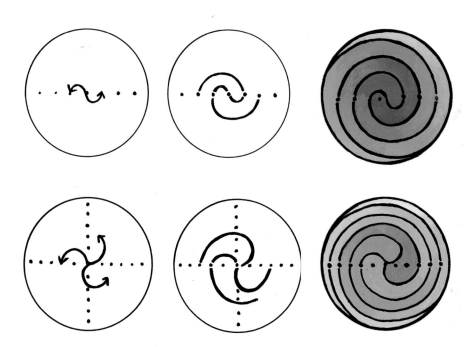

The single-coil spiral is found in many parts of the world, and had been unchanged for centuries until Celtic scribes adapted it by adding two, three or four coils.

The Triskele symbolised the sun in the Bronze Age. A variation can be seen in the Isle of Man's four-legged emblem.

Spirals connected in the shape of an S (above) are an adaptation of the three-legged Triskele.

Spirals joined in the shape of a C are late Celtic in style, with trumpet-shaped expansions.

Designing spirals

The method of execution for spiral designs is slightly different from that of knotwork. The grid is drawn into an equal number of segments but the design is completed by reversing the design on alternate segments. This method may seem complicated, but after a little practice you should find it comes naturally.

1. Draw a rough sketch of a section of your circular design – in this case a quarter.

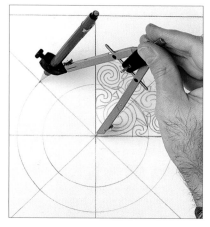

2. Draw a grid on a sheet of tracing paper and place the sketch underneath one section. Draw two guide circles with compasses.

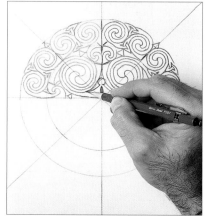

3. Trace the first segment. Reverse the sketch and complete the second segment.

4. The first half of the rough design completed.

5. The completed rough design.

6. Using sky blue and a touch of white, begin at the centre and start filling in the design using a No. 2 brush.

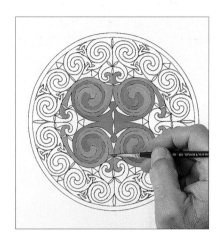

7. Add a touch of white to tone down some sections of the blue. Change to brilliant green blended with white and begin to build up the colours.

8. Still working outwards from the centre, gradually reduce the amount of blue used and bring in more green.

9. Add spectrum yellow to the mix and build up the design. Still using a No. 2 brush, gradually reduce the amount of green used as you work outwards.

10. Paint in the border using Bengal rose. Adding a touch of white will help to even up this colour, which can be a little patchy over large areas.

11. Change to a No. 000 brush and begin filling in the centre of the design using Bengal rose with a touch of yellow spectrum.

12. With undiluted Bengal rose, pick out details round the edge of the design. Change to black and fill in the final areas.

13. Outline the design with a technical pen.

The finished design.

Left: The Triskele spiral.

Below: A design adapted from a small section of a carpet page in the Book of Kells.

Spiral borders

Once you have chosen a design, the easiest way to begin is to consider how the corners will work. Some of the examples below could be adapted to work with similar patterns.

If you use tracing paper to overlay a corner, you should begin to see ways to align the border so that the movement of the pattern flows naturally without looking clumsy. Make sure you are completely happy with your design for the corner before continuing, so that you will not have second thoughts when you begin to paint the finished work and end up with a disappointing result.

When you have overcome this hurdle, you can begin to section up and trace out the rest of the border, segment by segment. If you need to stretch or compress the design to fit, it is best to do it from the spiral tails.

Tip

Any large spaces left between the spirals can be filled with triangles, circles and half-moon shapes.

Key Patterns

The key pattern is an elaboration of the Greek key or fret design. The earliest examples were discovered in Russia, carved on mammoth tusks dating from between 20,000 and 10,000 BC.

At first, key patterns were used mainly for borders. Later, Christian Celts developed them into complex, maze-like panels which featured strongly on stonework and manuscript decoration.

Key patterns played a significant part in Celtic design, especially in the Christian era, though this is often overlooked. The golden age for the key pattern was between the sixth and eight centuries when the scribes and stone carvers were at their most inventive. The style became progressively less popular, however, and it is unknown in late Celtic art.

It takes time to assimilate the complex structure of key patterns, but it is worth persevering as they are ultimately extremely rewarding. It is hoped these pages will encourage you to experiment further with key patterns, as they can look very dramatic and pleasing when completed.

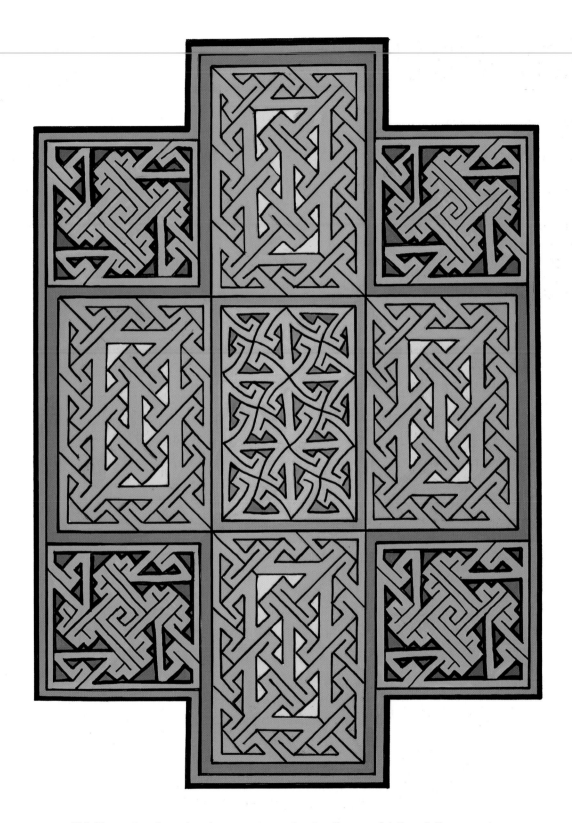

This illustration shows how key patterns can be visually powerful, though they are not as fluid as some of the other Celtic styles and are more suitable for borders and panels.

Designing key patterns

I have always found key patterns the most difficult to work with, and it does not surprise me that the style became progressively less popular before falling into disuse. The Celtic scribes worked out much of the initial design on wax tablets, but fortunately we have modern aids like tracing paper to make things a little easier.

1. The rough design, partly completed to show the different stages.

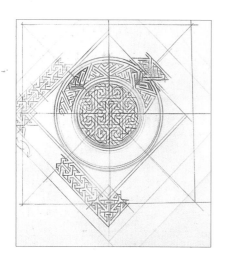

2. Draw a grid on a sheet of tracing paper, place it over the rough design and draw in guide circles.

3. The completed central pattern.

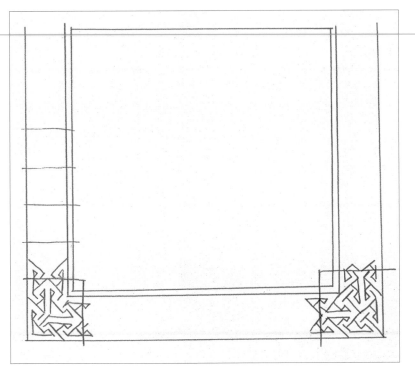

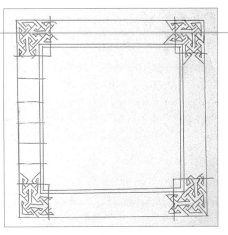

5. Complete the top corners and insert guidelines for the border grid, noting that the design will repeat in opposite corners.

4. On a separate piece of paper, draw a rough sketch of the lower corners of the outer border. The initial design has been simplified.

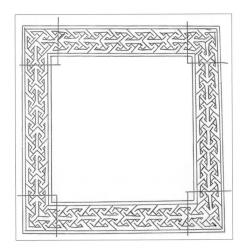

6. Repeat a section of the corner pattern in each border grid segment to build up the design.

7. The completed rough design, with border.

8. Mask the centre circle with layered strips of self-adhesive memo sheet.

9. Lay paper round the rest of the design to protect the background. With a toothbrush, flick on spatters of cerulean blue.

10. Build up the outlines of the central design with a technical pen.

11. Build up the central pattern using sky blue and red.

*The multicoloured stippled effect at the centre of the finished
design can also be seen in the illustrations on page 28.*

Key pattern borders

As with the other patterns, work out the corners first. Remember that the direction of the pattern on either side of the corner will probably be different, so your tracing will have to be flipped.

If you look at the borders opposite you will note that they move in opposite directions, so your template will need to be flipped over on alternate sides. This means there will be two different corner patterns, as you can see from the example below.

You may find that you are left with a small gap when you have worked your way round the border with the template. Do not panic; although Celtic patterns may look precise, it is in fact possible to cheat a little. Try extending or reducing the legs of the bands a little until they do fit. It is more than likely that the adjustment will be unnoticeable.

Although key pattern borders require patience and concentration, they can look extremely dramatic when completed and it is well worth persevering with the technicalities. Experiment by using shading moving from light to dark; with multicoloured effects; colouring detail in black to make the pattern appear to stand out in relief; or by flicking paint on the finished border to give a carved stone effect.

Tip

To keep your ideas fresh and flowing, do not be afraid to experiment with different ways of creating your pictures. Play with new materials and try to create your own, recognisable style of work.

The precise forms of key patterns require a little perseverance, but can produce an extremely dramatic effect.

Step patterns

These patterns resemble a flight of stairs: the lines are often arranged symmetrically round a centre, and shaded alternately light and dark. Step patterns appear very seldom in Christian Celtic art except on enamel bosses of metalwork. The resemblance of the designs to the carpet pages in the Lindisfarne Gospel leaves us in little doubt that the illuminators were greatly influenced by metalworkers and enamellers.

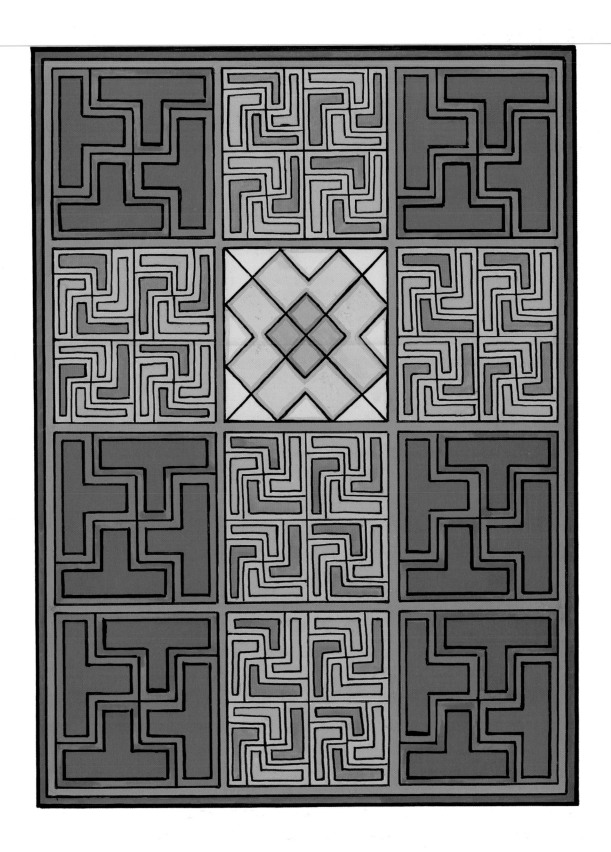

Zoomorphic Design

Zoomorphic ornament is based on animals, birds and reptiles, though in the hands of the Celtic artist nothing is as it seems: parts of different animals mingle and cats and dogs can have the bodies of birds. Anthropomorphic ornament is based on the human body, but both zoomorphic and anthropomorphic ornament may feature in the same design.

The seventh century Book of Durrow is the earliest surviving manuscript to feature elaborate zoomorphic ornamentation. Its decoration depicts long-snouted animals, similar to those found on artefacts from the Anglo-Saxon Sutton Hoo burial ship.

In the Gospel books, many animal symbols are used to represent Christ. The fish is the earliest Christian symbol for Christ and the soul; the snake and the lion represent the resurrection, and the peacock signifies Christ's incorruptibility. Dogs symbolise fidelity and there is also the image of a sheepdog guiding the flock.

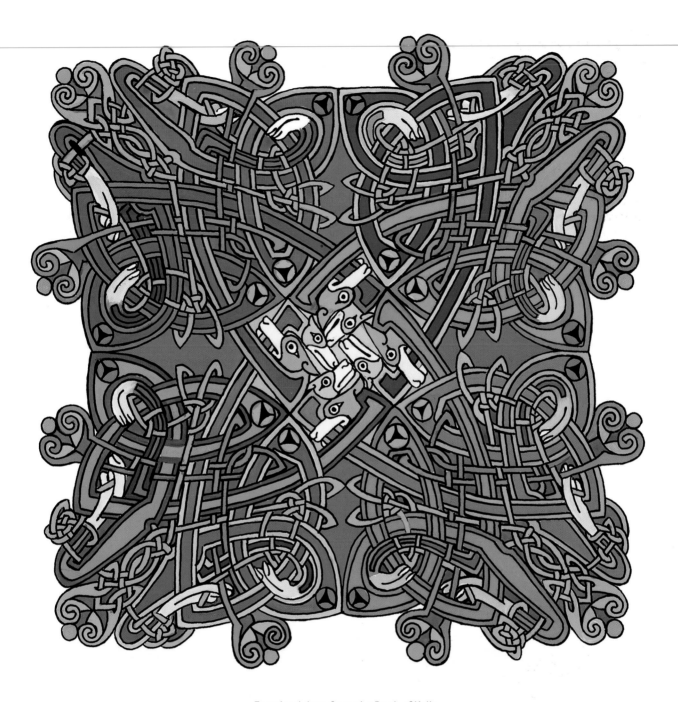

Entwined dogs from the Book of Kells.

Zoomorphic ornament

Zoomorphic ornament is wonderful. The more intricate it is the better, especially when it comes to the finishing touches and the feathers, body parts and claws need to be decorated. You can spend hours moving around torn-off strips of tracing paper, each featuring, for example, a dog, cat, bird or man, trying to find some new way of interlacing them. Once the idea is in place you can start to work on the details, creating the under and over movements and stretching limbs, necks and beaks to fit your design. There are numerous examples in the pages of old manuscripts, and as you gain more confidence in your abilities you may even find yourself inventing your own strange, mythical beasts!

Tip

Anthropomorphic and zoomorphic designs can be extremely intricate, if you have the patience. Experiment with sections in different colours, or even sections which feature different animal or human forms.

Adding animals and birds to designs makes them even more complex, as these partly coloured designs show.

Designing zoomorphic patterns

Zoomorphic ornament can be used with any other kind of Celtic pattern work. It lends a mystical quality to any design, whether simple or painstakingly intricate. Sometimes it is not possible to create an absolutely correct interlace for a zoomorphic pattern. Do not be discouraged when this happens and you cannot find a solution to the problem. You can always go for a walk and then look at it again.

1. The initial sketch which will form a quarter of a repeat design.

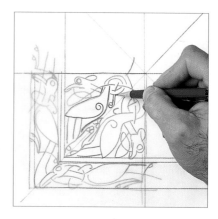

2. Draw up a grid on tracing paper. Insert the sketch beneath the grid and trace the design, refining details as you proceed.

3. Quarter of the rough border design completed.

4. Reverse the rough design and place it under the tracing paper as shown to provide a guide for the next segment of the design.

5. When completing the second segment, remember that fine details must be adjusted, especially where sections join, to ensure a consistent 'woven' effect.

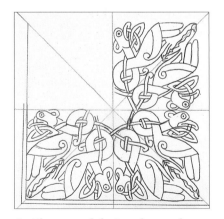

6. The central design shown three-quarters completed.

7. The finished rough design for the centre of the pattern.

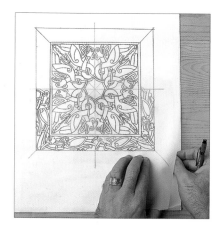

8. Trace the first corner of the border from the initial doodle.

9. A quarter of the border design has been completed.

10. Build up the design by moving the doodle round and repeating it. This border design does not need adjustment where the sections join.

11. The finished rough design, complete with border.

12. Start painting the design with Bengal rose and a No. 000 brush, lightening the colour with a touch of white towards the centre.

This simple zoomorphic design could be enhanced by adding more detail to the feathers, and outlining the neck and head with lighter or darker colours.

*The Eye of Sarph, above, shows how
the intricacy of knotwork makes it
particularly effective with zoomorphic or
anthropomorphic design.*

Zoomorphic borders

The strange birds and animals of zoomorphic ornament are particularly effective when used as borders. Let your imagination run riot, weaving the patterns in and out of legs and beaks; intertwine claws and add fearsome-looking talons or horns; incorporate wings decorated with intricate patterns.

Celtic Calligraphy

This chapter explores the art of formal writing, from the movement of the pen on the paper, to the sensual curves of the letterforms and the meanings of the words themselves. By developing your skills and confidence, and combining them with 'play' and experimentation, you can discover a seemingly endless source of creative and expressive possibilities for calligraphy. It is possible to give words a different meaning or emphasis simply by changing the way they are written – just as we can alter the spoken word by changing inflection.

We use the familiar abstract shapes that we call our alphabet on a daily basis often without thinking about their origin. They are the result of a long period of evolution, punctuated by periods of great beauty and consummate skill. It is to these roots and traditions that we should initially return for our calligraphy.

The isolated monastic life created centres of calligraphic and artistic expertise and produced books and documents essential to the life of a religious community. There would have been the daily ritual of quill cutting, vellum preparation, and pigment grinding and mixing, which resulted in the creation of manuscripts which were intended as a testament of faith and love of God by their makers.

Today, whilst we marvel at the beauty and skill displayed by the scribes and mourn the loss of the majority of manuscripts, decimated by Scandinavian raids, we can learn to recreate these letterforms in our own way, taking pride and pleasure in our work as we renew old skills, or take up the broad-edge pen for the first time.

This chapter lays the basic foundations for Celtic lettering and decoration, with an emphasis on the rich historical traditions behind our alphabet. Letter variations are also demonstrated, which can be practised once you have acquired some of the basic skills. These will lend a more contemporary look to your work.

Decorated Initial 'A'
Gouache on HP watercolour paper.

House Blessing
This piece of calligraphy incorporates decorated letters adapted from the great masterpieces of medieval art: the Book of Kells (Irish, seventh century), and the Lindisfarne Gospels (North-East England, late seventh century). It is worked on artificial parchment using non-waterproof Indian ink and gouache.

Materials and Equipment

The basic essentials for calligraphy are pens, paper and ink. Whilst the quill and reed pen were the original writing tools, manufactured pens are now readily available.

Pens

The selection of nibs and holders is very much a personal one. Pen holders are available in different materials and fit most nibs. There is a wide range of broad-edge fountain pens available; these are useful for practice and ephemeral pieces. Dip pens are really most suitable for formal calligraphy. While you are working and immediately you have finished, dip the pen into a **rinsing pot** as if you were filling with ink and wipe dry, preferably with a **cotton cloth**. You will also find black or coloured **technical drawing pens** useful for outlining and for tracing images.

Inks

Best results are obtained with a good quality non-waterproof **Indian ink**. This can benefit from the addition of a little **lamp black gouache** to make the ink denser, and **gum arabic** to reduce the risk of smudging once the ink is dry. There is now a wide range of coloured inks available in addition to black.

Paints

Gouache is ideal for decoration and writing in colour. This is available in an extensive range of colours and many more can be mixed from a basic palette. Artist's quality will give the best results. **Process white** is useful for correcting mistakes, and a few drops of **oxgall liquid** will assist the flow of gouache mixes.

Brushes

A small **children's paintbrush** is inexpensive and ideal for mixing colours and filling the pen. For painting, use a good quality **kolinsky sable**. These brushes have a very good point for detailed work. The size determines the amount of paint the brush will hold. A No. 1 will suit most purposes, though for painting larger areas a No. 4 or No. 8 is recommended.

Coloured pencils

Watercolour pencils are useful for colouring motifs.

Palette

Ceramic palettes are best for mixing colours in. The container needs to be white, so that you can see the true value of your colours. Decant ink into a **shallow container** and support this with foam to prevent it from tipping when you are working.

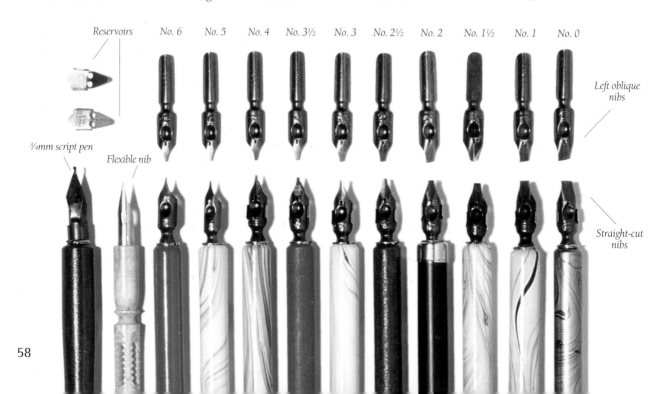

Reservoirs   No. 6   No. 5   No. 4   No. 3½   No. 3   No. 2½   No. 2   No. 1½   No. 1   No. 0

Left oblique nibs

¾mm script pen   Flexible nib   Straight-cut nibs

Paper

Even practice paper needs to produce sharp lettering, and **layout paper** is very good for this purpose. For finished work, there is an enormous range of lovely papers to choose from. **Cartridge paper** is probably the cheapest. **Pastel paper** is available in a range of colours, and **watercolour paper** is also very good. Watercolour paper should have a hot pressed (HP) finish which provides a smooth surface for writing. The **Indian handmade papers** are popular for calligraphy because of their subtle colours and textures. **Scrap paper** and **tracing paper** are always useful and strips of **black card** are invaluable for setting margins.

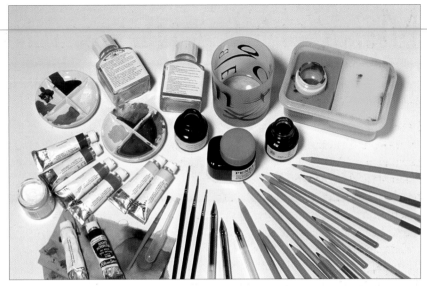

Various pens, inks, paints and associated equipment.

Drawing equipment

It is essential to have some means of measuring and ruling guidelines for writing. A pair of **lockable dividers** and a **parallel ruler** (not pictured) would be ideal, a 460mm (18in) **T-square** or **ruler** would be a suitable alternative. A large **set square** is used for ruling in margins. You will also need **pencils** of varying hardness for ruling lines and tracing illustrations. A **sandpaper block** will keep them sharp. **Propelling pencils**, and their **leads** are a convenient alternative. Two pencils taped together form a double-edged writing tool, used for

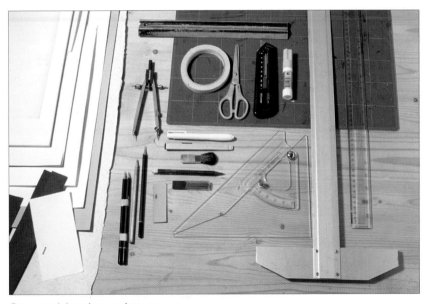

Paper and drawing equipment.

learning the principles of the broad-edge pen, and for drawing larger letters. Lines are erased after writing, and a **soft brush** will deal with the debris. **Scissors**, **cutting mat**, **craft knife**, **metal ruler**, **masking tape** and **repositionable glue** have all been used later in this chapter.

Drawing board

Commercially available drawing boards can be purchased, but it is also possible to construct one yourself. Alternatively, you can use a sheet of hardboard approximately 61 x 46cm (24 x 18in). This can rest on your lap and form the required angle against the edge of the table, or be propped against a pile of books. Whichever method you use, the board will need to be covered with about eight sheets of an inexpensive **drawing paper** and a final layer of **blotting paper** to provide a sympathetic writing surface.

Basic Principles

You need to understand how the script you are studying is constructed before you can produce it. Examples are provided as a guide to how the script should look, but these are not intended to be copied slavishly. The aim is to capture the spirit of the script; copying without understanding can produce results which lack the strength of the original.

It is important to learn the formation of the letters to enable you to write fluently and accurately. Begin by familiarising yourself with the equipment and principles of penmanship in order to achieve a greater understanding of the scripts concerned. These basic principles are applicable whichever calligraphic style you choose to study later.

There are two main characteristics of broad-pen lettering: the first is that thick and thin strokes are brought about by the use of a broad-edge pen held at an angle to a horizontal writing line; the second is that letters are generally built up from a sequence of strokes with the pen travelling in a left to right, and top to bottom direction. There are not usually any joining strokes (ligatures) between broad-pen letters, unlike handwriting which is more economical in terms of movement to achieve the necessary speed.

The finished pen-made letter is the product of three variables known as weight, angle and form.

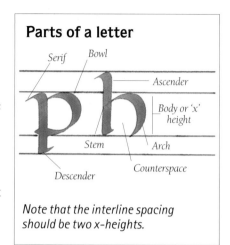

Parts of a letter

Serif · Bowl · Ascender · Body or 'x' height · Stem · Arch · Descender · Counterspace

Note that the interline spacing should be two x-heights.

Weight

Whether the texture of a script appears overall to be heavy or light is determined by the ratio between the width of the nib and the height of the writing line. Nowadays, this is most often referred to as the x-height, a term borrowed from typography.

Heavyweight letter 3 nib widths

Lightweight letter 10 nib widths

Angle

Because the pen has a broad edge, the angle that this edge makes to the writing line will affect the shape of the pen stroke. The pen angle controls the distribution of the weight around the letters, and it should be consistent throughout the pen strokes. Most scripts have a specified pen angle.

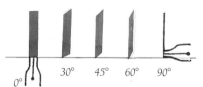

0° · 30° · 45° · 60° · 90°

The flatter the pen angle the fatter the vertical line becomes. This has a profound effect on the shape of letters

0° · 45° · 90°

Form

All calligraphic letters have an underlying structure or form which is usually based on the shape of the 'O'. This letter is sometimes referred to as 'the mother of the alphabet'. This shape is common to other letters and thus unifies the alphabet.

Uncial form, slightly wider than its height

Roundhand, based on two overlapping circles

Italic form, based on an oval, often with a forward slant

Ruling up

Ruling up parallel guidelines for your writing is an essential but often neglected element of calligraphy. To help you write fluently and consistently, guidelines should be precisely measured and drawn using a well-sharpened pencil or propelling pencil. An HB hardness will allow you to rule lightly without scoring the paper, and will be easy to erase later. Always start with a larger sheet of paper than needed and allow generous margins. Double check your measurements, and for finished work, rule up some spare sheets in case of mistakes.

Tip

Ensure that you have a good light source when you are working – either a window, or a daylight bulb in a desk lamp. If you are right-handed, the light should be directed from the left; if left-handed, from the right.

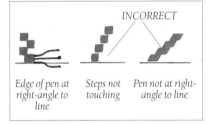

INCORRECT

Edge of pen at right-angle to line | Steps not touching | Pen not at right-angle to line

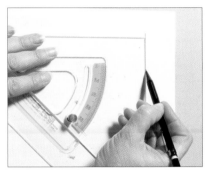

1. Rule a line at the top of the paper then use a set square to rule lines on the left- and right-hand sides. This will give you your margins to work within.

2. Make a note of the nib size on spare paper for future reference. Use your nib to mark four steps, ensuring that the nib is exactly at right angles to the horizontal and that the steps are touching.

3. Place a small paper strip next to the steps and mark off the top and bottom points. (You could use dividers to measure this if you prefer.)

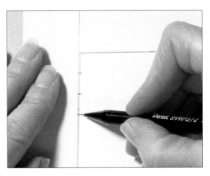

4. Use the marks on the paper strip made in step 3 to mark the x-height down both vertical margins, starting from the top ruled line. Continue down the page for the required number of lines. If you are using dividers, 'walk' them down the page, pricking the paper as you go.

5. Use a ruler and pencil to draw lines across the paper, joining up the marks. If the interline spacing is two x-heights, then you can miss out every third set of marks.

Using a pencil

This demonstration is designed to help you learn about the shapes of letters before weight is added with the broad-edge pen. Once you have traced them from the exemplar, you can copy them freehand. You need to practise these letters using an HB pencil – this is responsive to use, but it loses its point very quickly.

All alphabets should be considered as a carefully matching set of letters where the basis of its design is usually the letter 'O'. This letter determines the shape and proportions of the other letters. Understanding the skeleton form will help with the letter variations later in this chapter.

1. Use a craft knife to take off the wood at the top of your pencil, leaving about 12mm (½in) of lead showing.

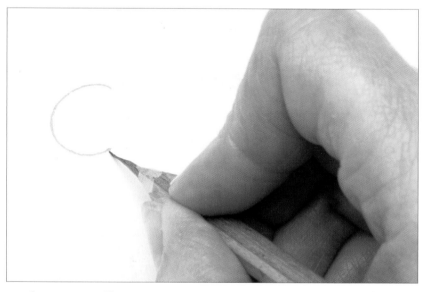

2. Roll the lead on sandpaper to produce a point. Repeat as soon as the point begins to disappear when you are working.

3. Place a piece of layout paper over the exemplar and secure it in place with masking tape. Trace off the letters so that you begin to learn their shapes, proportions and relationships to one another.

4. Rule up lines approximately the same width apart as the exemplar. Use the same method as shown on page 61.

5. Practise the letters freehand, copying from the exemplar. Work from top to bottom and from left to right in preparation for working with a pen.

6. When you feel confident, reduce the size of the letters and experiment with writing out whole words and sentences.

Skeleton exemplar

This form is based on a circle which is slightly wider than its height. The grid, shown in red, is a square – when the letters are drawn with their sides just outside the box, they will be the correct width. The letters are in groups of related shapes rather than in alphabetical order. The same strokes recur, therefore instead of writing rows of the same letter, work through in this order, and each letter will reinforce the next. Follow the order and direction of the arrows when drawing the letters.

Round letters

Tops are flattened slightly and letters are narrower than 'O'

Ascender and bowl aligned on left

Small bowl letters

Upper bowls of 'B' and 'S' are smaller than the bottom. All bowls relate to 'O' shape. 'S' is aligned on the right-hand side

Arched letters

Descender aligned on left

Arches relate to the shape of 'O'

Straight letters

  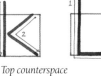

Top counterspace smaller than bottom

Arms aligned on right side

Cross over above centre, making top counterspace smaller than bottom

First stroke slightly narrower than third

Diagonal letters

This shows a practical application of the skeleton form on dark blue card using white gouache and a script pen. Counterspaces are filled using gouache.

Using a pen

Before starting to write, you need to familiarise yourself with the action of a broad-edge pen which may be quite different to anything you have written with before. It can also take a little while to become accustomed to filling the pen fairly frequently – the reservoir does not hold a great deal of ink, and a broad nib will exhaust this quite quickly.

You may find it useful to trace the letters from the exemplar a couple of times to familiarise yourself with the shape. Take care to match the pen angle to achieve the right distribution of weight, and follow the order and direction of strokes.

Tip

If you are left-handed, you may find it easier to work with the paper at an angle.

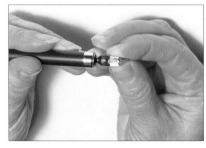

1. Push the nib into the holder as far as it will go. Make sure that it goes between the claws and the outer edge of the barrel.

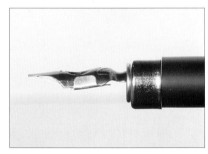

2. Slide the reservoir on to the nib. It should feel firm and the nib should not move about. The reservoir should be tight enough not to fall off, but not so tight that it impedes the nib's flexibility.

3. Ensure the reservoir is in the correct position, approximately 2mm ($\frac{1}{12}$in) from the end of the nib and touching the underneath of the nib. The metal is quite flexible and can be adjusted accordingly.

4. Decant the ink into a small, shallow container supported with foam to prevent it from tipping over. Fill the pen by dipping it into the ink no further than the holes in the reservoir. Alternatively, you can load a brush with ink and then stroke it over the reservoir.

5. Move the pen from side to side on a piece of scrap paper to encourage the ink to flow (this is called 'the calligrapher's wiggle'!). You will need to do this whenever you fill the pen, to ensure that it is not overloaded.

6. You are now ready to start writing! Remember to use a guard sheet under your hand to protect the paper as you write.

Exemplar showing pen strokes

The comments on the skeleton exemplar (see page 63) also apply to the pen form. Try and memorise the shape and construction of the letter so that you do not have to look away as you write. Compare each letter with the model and not the last letter that you wrote, or you may repeat your mistakes. Work through all the letters as before, to be sure of reaching 'Z', then none are neglected.

The second stroke overlaps the first – this applies to most of the pen strokes and helps give the writing its strength and solidity

Pen angle is 20° (equivalent to just after ten past on a clock face)

Letters are four nib-widths high

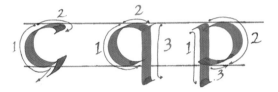

Pause and turn just before the base line

Increase pen angle to 40° for this stroke

Second stroke of 'H' and third stroke of 'M' should just cut the base line

Alternative form of 'Y'

Alternative form of 'W' shown on last line

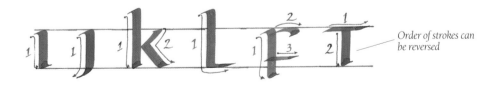

Order of strokes can be reversed

Increase pen angle to 40° for these strokes

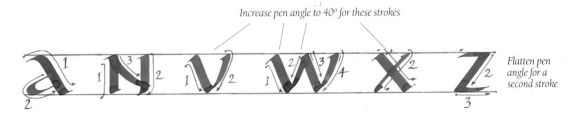

Flatten pen angle for a second stroke

Words and Sentences

Once you have learned the formation of the letters and practised the shapes a few times, use them in combinations of words and sentences rather than producing rows and rows of the same letter.

Tip

Using your writing in small finished pieces will teach you other aspects of the craft in addition to the lettering. Calligraphy is a skill which improves with use, so commonplace items such as envelopes, letters and greetings cards are a useful means of putting theory into practice.

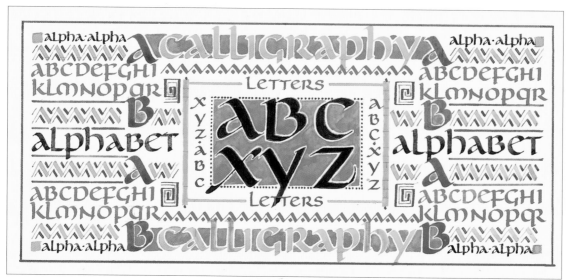

Alphabet sampler

This sampler is written in gouache using ten different pens. It illustrates the variations in letter size which can be achieved.

Birth Celebration

Written and painted with gouache, on dark blue Ingres paper. Large and small nib sizes bring contrast and dominance to a simple design.

Letter spacing

Letters need to be positioned so that the overall pattern of writing appears evenly balanced. This is achieved when the space inside the letter is balanced by the space either side of it. Because of the variations in letter shapes, this cannot be an exact science, but 'rule of thumb' guides are always useful to a beginner. Two adjacent vertical strokes should have about two thirds of the width of the counterspace of 'N' between them. Because of its shape, a round stroke should be a little closer to an adjacent vertical, and two round strokes closer again.

NI NO OO

To help you develop an eye for balanced spacing, practise words which combine these strokes.

ONION

It is often easier to assess your spacing when you are not able to read the words, so try viewing your writing from a distance or upside down.

An adjustment needs to be made for letters with open counterspaces, otherwise this space visually adds to the letter space and can create 'holes' in the text.

c e c s l f t a x z

Word spacing

Too much space between words will create vertical 'rivers' of white in a page of writing. Allow no more than the width of 'N' between words.

ather picks up quartz an
els my grandfather pick
her picks up quartz and valuable
er picks up quartz and valuable
picks up quartz and valuable onyx
cks up quartz and valuable onyx jew
cks up quuartz and valuable onyx jewels my
able onyx jewels my grandfather picks up
up quartz and valuable onyx jewels my grandf
wels my grandfather picks up quartz and valuab
artz and valuable onyx jewels my grandfather picks up quartz an
z and valuable onyx jewels my grandfather picks up quartz
and valuable onyx jewels my grandfather picks up quartz and valuable
yx jewels my grandfather picks up quartz and valuable onyx jewels my

Alphabet sentences

These alphabet sentences were written to practise letterform and spacing. Small writing can actually be more difficult than large, so reduce the nib size gradually as shown here.

Celtic Decoration

Much Celtic decoration was based on interlacing knotwork, spirals and key patterns (see Chapter 1). In keeping with a more simplistic and contemporary style, these can be adapted and used as borders, motifs or in the stems and bowls of letters.

The letters and borders on the following pages can be enlarged or reduced on a photocopier and traced using the method shown here.

Knotwork

A Celtic knot is made up of one or more strands, and each 'under' must be followed by an 'over' to interlace the strands of the knot. Knotwork can be made to appear three-dimensional by using simple shading techniques, as demonstrated here.

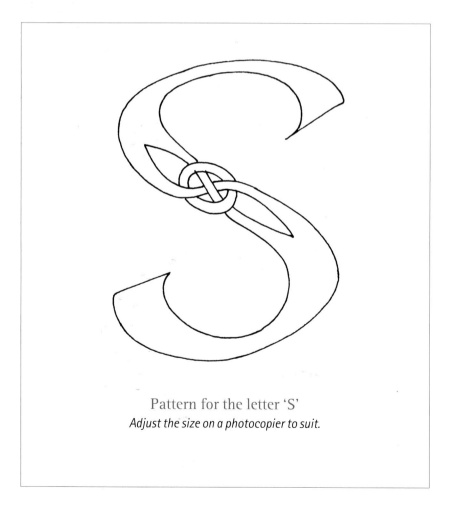

Pattern for the letter 'S'
Adjust the size on a photocopier to suit.

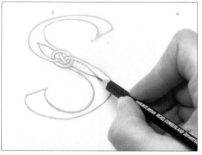

1. Place a piece of tracing paper over the letter and secure in place with masking tape. Trace around the outline with a hard pencil.

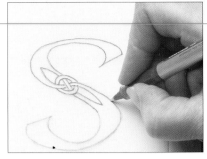

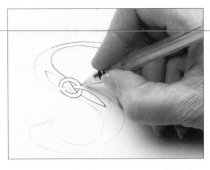

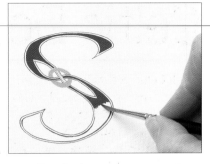

2. Turn the tracing over and go over the back of it with a soft pencil. Now turn it the right way up again and place in position. Secure with masking tape. Go around the outline with a coloured pen to transfer the image. Check it has transferred before removing the tracing.

3. Outline the letter using a black technical pen. Leave to dry before erasing the pencil line.

4. Fill in the knot using a No. 1 brush and pale purple gouache. Fill in the letter using purple gouache. Leave a white moat between the colour and the outline.

Knot painted flat

Knot painted with shading

5. Use white gouache to add highlights to the knot where the strands pass over one another. Add shadows where the strands go underneath using a darker tone of purple.

6. Outline the knot with a black technical pen. Touch up the rest of the outline if necessary, to complete the letter.

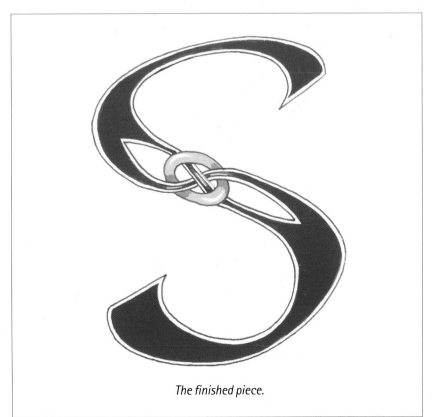

The finished piece.

Letters

The simplest form of decorated letter is traditionally written larger than the main text, with the counterspace filled in with a contrasting colour, and the whole letter surrounded by a border of red dots.

Here, the basic shape of 'A', 'B', 'C', 'F', 'H' and 'R' were constructed using two pencils taped together to form a double-edged writing tool. All the letters are painted with gouache, in traditional and contemporary colour combinations.

Some of the designs could be adapted for other letters, and they can also be reduced or enlarged on a photocopier.

Motifs

The construction of selected motifs is here demonstrated with coloured pens for illustrative purposes. In practice, you should use pencil, which can be erased after the decoration has been drawn and outlined as shown on pages 68–69. The Triskele knot shown below is a simple knot based on a triangle.

Triskele knot

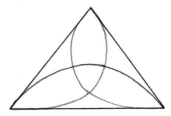  

1. Draw three curved lines into the corners of a triangular framework which can have any proportions.

2. Double up on the lines to form strands. There should be a gap in the centre.

3. Weave the strands, ensuring each 'over' is followed by an 'under'. After outlining, erase the pencil and colour with watercolour pencils. The knot can be used with or without a background.

These motifs use combinations of the Triskele knot. They are variously painted with gouache, watercolour and watercolour pencils.

Heart-twining knot

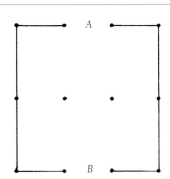

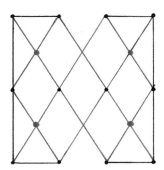

1. Mark out a rectangular grid of 3 x 2 units, placing a dot at the corner of each unit.

2. Draw walls around, leaving the units at A and B open.

3. Place a dot in the centre of each rectangle and draw a diagonal grid (shown in red).

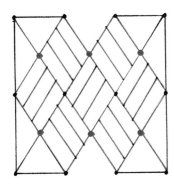

4. Draw a strand (green) inside and narrower than the diagonal grid. Strands in adjacent units go in the opposite direction to each other.

5. Join the strands up. When they reach a wall, they are deflected through 90°, and make a U-turn at the corners. Two rules are changed here – the corners are rounded and not pointed, and the strand goes through the openings at A and B to form a point.

6. When you have made two hearts from a continuous strand, draw in the outline, erase the pencil lines and colour with watercolour pencils. Wet the pencil to achieve a darker shade.

Variation on heart-twining knot

The two hearts in the knot above are made from a continuous strand. In the variation here, two separate strands are entwined. This design is created by placing a wall at A–B, deflecting the strand through approximately 70° and breaking it.

Borders

Knotwork borders are based on a square or rectangular grid. When designing a border, divide the length required into a whole number of units. The basic grid shown below can be extended to fit any length, width or shape.

Basic grid

 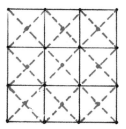 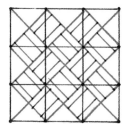  

1. Draw a square of 3 x 3 units. Place a dot at the corner of each unit.

2. Place a dot in the centre of each of the nine units and draw a diagonal grid (pink).

3. Draw a strand (green) inside and narrower than the diagonal square. Strands in adjacent squares go in the opposite direction to each other.

4. Join the strands up. When a strand reaches a wall it is deflected through 90°; when it enters a corner, it makes a pointed U-turn.

5. Complete the motif by colouring with gouache and filling in a black background.

Variations on the basic grid

1. Place walls at intervals within a rectangle to vary the pattern and make a larger, more interesting area of interlaced knotwork.

2. Draw the strands (green) within the diagonal grid (pink) as before.

3. Join the strands up and deflect through 90° at each wall (black). Corners are made in the same way as in the basic grid above.

4. Complete the border then paint with yellow, light blue and green. Add an indigo background.

Figure-of-eight knot pattern

1. Mark the centre of a rectangle.

2. Draw a figure of eight so that it crosses in the centre.

3. Draw a circle in the centre.

4. Double up on the strands, adjusting the drawn cross in the centre.

5. Sort out the 'overs' and 'unders'.

6. Colour the single motif with watercolour pencils.

7. Repeat, and join up motifs to form a continuous strand.

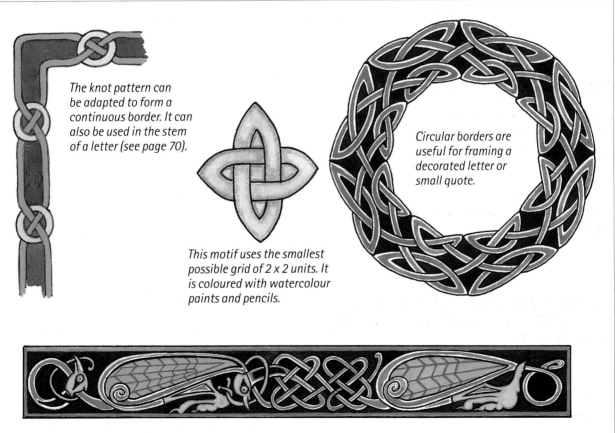

The knot pattern can be adapted to form a continuous border. It can also be used in the stem of a letter (see page 70).

This motif uses the smallest possible grid of 2 x 2 units. It is coloured with watercolour paints and pencils.

Circular borders are useful for framing a decorated letter or small quote.

This border incorporates birds adapted from the Lindisfarne Gospels. They are thought to represent the cormorants seen in the area.

Layout

Even a simple greeting on a card requires planning, so that the writing looks attractive and visually balanced against the size and shape of the card.

There are various types of layout which can be used, and the best option is arrived at by a process of 'cut and paste'. This then provides a blueprint for the finished piece. Even large and complex calligraphic panels can be seen to contain a combination of more simple arrangements.

The amount of white space around the work is vital to the visual balance of the design. Margins which are too small make the writing appear too cramped. The amount of space needed around the work is related to the space within, i.e. light writing would need more space around it. Layouts should always be assessed by placing strips of card around the work as shown. Doing this will often show up unbalanced areas of the design which might otherwise go unnoticed.

As a general rule, the strong horizontal character of uncials needs generous interline spacing of twice the x-height. The purpose of the interline spacing is to emphasise the horizontal lines for ease of reading. The amount allowed will depend upon the weight, size and quantity of text. Short lines of writing need less interline space than long ones.

1. Write the text in your chosen pen size. Photocopy four times.

2. Number the lines on the photocopies. Take one copy and place it on a cutting mat. Cut the text into lines using a craft knife and ruler, or use scissors.

3. Rule a generous left-hand margin on to layout paper. Mark and rule guide lines, using the same ruling as your original text. Assemble the strips into the first layout shown opposite. Glue in place using a repositionable glue stick or roller.

4. Erase all the pencil marks. Put margins around your work and use this frame to check how the arrangement works. Repeat steps 2–4 with the other layouts. When you have decided upon a layout, transfer the measurements and copy the text on to good paper, following your chosen format.

Types of layout

The choice of text will often make some decisions for you. For instance, the example used here is better suited to a horizontal format (sometimes known as landscape). If a vertical (or portrait) format had been required, the lines would have been divided to make them shorter, thereby increasing the number of lines. Although this arrangement might be satisfactory visually, it could impair the flow of the words when being read.

mary, mary, quite contrary,
how does your garden grow?
with silver bells and cockle shells
and pretty maids all in a row.

Ranged left

This is the easiest layout. All lines start from a vertical left-hand margin. Alternate lines can be indented as a variation of this layout.

mary, mary, quite contrary,
how does your garden grow?
with silver bells and cockle shells
and pretty maids all in a row.

Centred

Lines of text are equally balanced around a central vertical line. The writing needs to be reproduced carefully and exactly for the finished piece.

mary, mary, quite contrary,
how does your garden grow?
with silver bells and cockle shells
and pretty maids all in a row.

Ranged right

All lines finish at a vertical right-hand margin. Again, accuracy is needed when writing as a finished piece.

mary, mary, quite contrary,
how does your garden grow?
with silver bells and cockle shells
and pretty maids all in a row.

Asymmetric

This layout is freer and less formal in character. Although there is a strong central vertical axis, no two lines begin and end in the same place, and they are visually balanced around the axis.

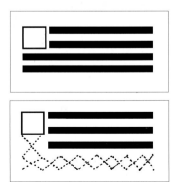

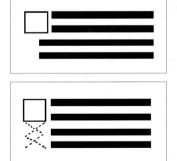

These line drawings show the possible positions for a decorated initial.

Contemporary Uncials

The beauty and rhythm of the uncial hand can be extended by developing variations of the basic script. These variations may be more appropriate in freer, more informal work, whilst still retaining the essential uncial character.

Variations are based on alterations to the weight, angle and form (see page 60). You should be able to write the basic script confidently before you attempt this exercise. Work in a logical sequence without changing too many things at once.

Changing weight

The weight refers to the thickness of stroke relative to the height of the letter. Here the underlying form is unchanged (the skeleton form is on the left and in black). The weight has been progressively increased from left to right by using larger pens. The counterspace decreases as the weight increases.

Lightweight

Normal weight

Heavyweight

Changing form and weight

Here, the normally slightly wide circle has been laterally compressed. Each letter of the alphabet has to be treated in the same way to maintain the essential family resemblance. The x-height is five nib widths which allows more white space inside the letter.

Original form, with 22° pen angle

Laterally compressed form, with 22° pen angle

Note that flatter is fatter! A flat pen angle gives a wider vertical stroke (see page 60). The same principle can apply to the letters: narrow compressed forms are often written with a steeper pen angle.

Changing form and pen angle

The main difference here is that the arch is a branching arch made in one movement following the downstroke. It does not involve a pen lift and separate stroke as before. The pen angle is higher to accommodate this action. The shape is subtly changed to a softer oval, but the letters do not slant.

30° pen angle

Italicised variations

The italic form lends itself to the widest possible range of variations, from compressed to extended, light to heavyweight. This italicised variation has a lower branching arch and the 'O' form has been adjusted to match this shape. The letters have a slant of 5° from the vertical, which gives a more informal appearance.

40° pen angle

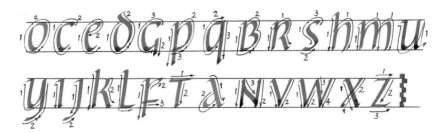

20° pen angle

jackdaws love my big sphinx of quartz

jackdaws love my big sphinx of quartz

22° pen angle

jackdaws love my big sphinx of quartz

Alternative letterforms for use with contemporary uncials

Moving away from the traditional uncial alphabet allows for some variations to individual letters. This allows you to achieve greater freedom of style and create a contemporary look.

Variations with colour

Blocks of text provide a wonderful opportunity to experiment with colour, as these examples show.

Texture

Lightweight open and mediumweight compressed variations create two very different textures when written in quantity.

Colour change

This gradual colour change is achieved by feeding subsequent colours into the pen before the previous one is exhausted, and without cleaning the pen.

Wet into Wet

These letters were written with turquoise calligraphy ink, then, while the ink was still wet, magenta was touched in with a brush. The counterspaces were painted with dilute mixtures of the colours.

Layering

This very diluted Payne's gray watercolour background was overwritten with turquoise and red calligraphy ink, when dry.

Celtic Knotwork Jewellery

Celtic knot designs can be found illustrating manuscripts, carved in wood and stone, enamelled and etched on to metal, impressed into clay, embroidered on to cushions, batiked and printed on to fabric and even burned as designs in wood. However, it is impossible to find a three-dimensional Celtic knot actually tied with cord or string.

The question is, therefore, did real Celtic knots ever exist in the past? We shall never know, as the cords and string that would have been used to make them would not have survived the passage of time. However, there are many ancient decorative knots in existence which definitely are Celtic in style, being interlaced and plaited in a very similar way. They are very attractive and yet are relatively unknown to artists and teachers in closely allied fibre arts such as weaving, crochet and macramé. They certainly deserve to be revived and used with the colourful cords and beautiful beads that are so readily available today.

Until now, these knots could only be found in books and journals for sailors and dedicated knot-tyers. In this chapter, the descriptions of how to tie them have been simplified and used to re-create Celtic knots in three dimensions which are perfect for the creation of surprisingly modern, stylish jewellery.

Opposite

This necklace (see pages 126–127) combines a Celtic square knot with Celtic beads and a circular pendant.

Materials and Equipment

Cords

Cords are available in several different materials, including nylon, leather and cotton. It is better to use a cord at least 1mm (1/24in) in diameter to show up the decorative knot; for jewellery a 2mm (1/12in) diameter cord is the thickest you will need. There is a special satin cord made especially for decorative knotting, which comes in many colours and looks smooth and silky although it is made from nylon or rayon. It has the perfect requirements for knotting: it is not too stiff, but firm enough to hold the shape of a loop without flopping. A good quality one will stand up to a good deal of handling without spoiling the appearance, a very important requirement for making elegant jewellery.

A selection of cords.

Beads, pendants and findings

There are numerous beautiful beads available, both in bead shops and by mail order. One very important thing to look out for when ordering by mail is determining the size of the hole: is it large enough for the cord you intend to use? Pendants often have larger holes and loops to suspend them and there is a huge variety available. The same goes for findings. Since knotted jewellery tends to be bold in style, the chunkier, more unusual findings usually suit it better.

Beads or old necklaces can also be bought from second-hand and charity shops. It is a matter of luck what you find, but there are some unusual pieces out there waiting to be discovered! Market stalls have some original ethnic jewellery and beads that are just asking to be combined with beautifully bold and colourful knots.

Other items

Scissors Your scissors need to be good quality and very sharp to give a clean cut to the cord so that it is easy to thread through the beads.

PVA glue This is very good for stiffening the ends of the cords, making a stiff 'needle' to thread through the beads. It is also useful for strengthening the finished Celtic knots. If you paint on a diluted solution (one part glue to nine parts water), it will not darken the colour too much.

Paintbrush For painting on the PVA glue. Buy a good enough quality not to shed hairs on to your handiwork.

Sticky tape Transparent tape is used to stiffen the ends of the cord to put through beads with large holes.

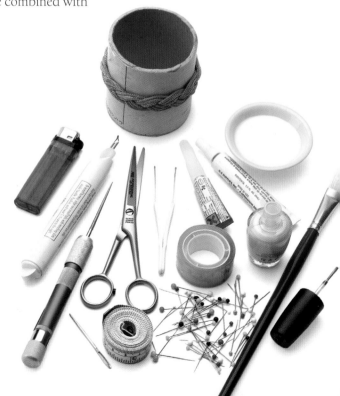

This method is quick and easy but it does increase the thickness of the cord end.

Lighter This is used to seal the ends of synthetic cord to stop it fraying.

Thread zapper This fairly new product works well on thinner synthetic cords. It is battery operated and quickly heats up to cut and seal the cord in one go, giving a very neat, clean finish.

Cork mat Ideal for pinning your knot in progress as you follow the knot pattern. Use a beanbag tray with a piece of cork attached to it as it is easy to keep at a comfortable angle for working on.

Pins Used with the cork mat.

Tweezers Fine tweezers can be very useful for pulling cords through narrow gaps. They must have rounded ends and a gentle gripping surface to grip the cord without damaging it.

Instant glue gel The gel type of instant glue is easier to control than the liquid. A tiny droplet of glue gel holds the cord in place and will not spread on to surrounding cords, discreetly securing your finished knot.

Epoxy glue Useful for general jewellery tasks like gluing rhinestones or brooch backs.

Bead reamer This is so useful! Two needle files and a 45° hole smoother are stored in the handle for when you need to enlarge and smooth the bead hole. Do not forget to clean the filing surface frequently with an old toothbrush to keep it working efficiently.

Needle A tapestry needle with a large hole and a smooth, blunt end is very useful for weaving the cords over and under each other, and also for threading the cords back through a button knot to finish a necklace.

Pliers and wire cutters Although we are working mainly with cords, pliers are very useful for dealing with findings. Two pairs of needle-nosed pliers are needed for opening jump rings, wire cutters are required for shortening headpins and round-nosed pliers are needed for creating round loops in wire for earrings or pendants.

Nail polish Very useful for stiffening the ends of cords for threading when the ends do not need to be very stiff. Quicker drying than PVA glue.

Cardboard cylinder A 7cm (2¾in) diameter piece of cardboard tubing cut from a tube (normally used to mail posters) is approximately wrist size and is used to make bangles and bracelets.

Tape measure Use this to ensure that you start off with enough cord to finish a project.

An array of beautiful beads. Some beads can be bought as necklaces and re-used for your own designs.

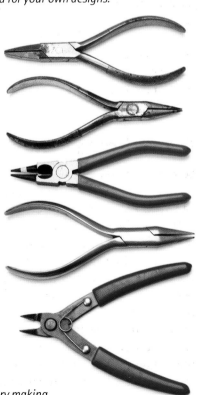

Pliers and wire cutters used for jewellery making.

Preparing Cords

Before you start making projects, you need to learn how to prepare cords.

Calculating lengths of cord

One of the most puzzling things to work out before you start a knotted project is how much cord will be needed to complete it. Often the cord required is much longer than you would have imagined. For example, the Turk's Head bangle on page 102 is made around a cardboard cylinder that is less than 7.5cm (3in) in diameter. Yet the amount of cord required to make the bangle is actually about 3m (118in); much more than you would think. The average length of a short necklace is approximately 45cm (18in) and the length of a long necklace is at least 70cm (28in). However, for both of these you should start with 3m (118in) of cord, as at least 30cm (12in) of extra cord will be needed to be able to tie the last knot on each side. So it is better to err on the long side to be sure of being able to finish the project.

If you see some particularly lovely cord but are not sure which project you will use it for, always buy at least 3m (118in) to be sure of having enough. Details of the length of cord needed are given at the beginning of each project.

Necklace lengths

The following table lists the average length of different types of necklace.

Choker	40cm	(16in)
Necklace with fastener	45cm	(18in)
Necklace without fastener	70cm	(28in)

Cord lengths for knots

The following table shows the approximate length of 2mm (1/12in) cord required to tie single knots.

Button knot	8.5cm	(3½in)
Sliding button knot	9.5cm	(3¾in)
Double button knot	25cm	(10in)

The following table shows how to determine the total length of 2mm (1/12in) cord required to make an 80cm (32in) necklace with one double button knot, ten single button knots and two sliding button knots.

Length of necklace	80cm	(32in)
Double button knot	25cm	(10in)
Ten button knots	85cm	(34in)
Two sliding knots	19cm	(7½in)
Allowance for tying the sliding knots	60cm	(24in)
Total length	269cm	(107½in)

It is better to have too much than too little, so add a small allowance for possible additions and cut a 3m (118in) length of cord.

Cutting and sealing cord ends

The cord will be easier to thread if the end has been cut on the diagonal with a sharp pair of scissors.

The cord ends need to be sealed to prevent fraying and as they are too thick to thread on a needle, they must be stiff enough to be able to pass through a bead easily. In a way, you will be transforming the end of the cord into its own stiff needle. There are several ways of doing this. The preferred method is to saturate the end with PVA glue, as shown. If the hole in the bead is uneven it is possible to cut a thin slice off the side of the stiffened cord end to make it thinner, to coax it through the bead.

The second method is to use nail polish to stiffen the ends. It is not as stiff as PVA but dries quickly and is good enough if the holes are nice and large.

Use a small paintbrush to apply the PVA glue to the cord. Use as much glue as the cord will absorb, all around, and up to 2.5cm (1in) from each end of the cord. Support the wet ends so they are not touching anything, then leave them to dry for at least an hour (longer for slow-drying glues) until the ends are very hard. Now cut the ends again to make sharp, needle-like points.

Sealing the cord end with nail polish.

Sticky tape is another quick method, but it makes the ends thicker, so the holes must be larger than the cord thickness to allow the cord through.

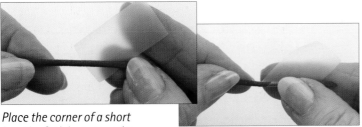

Place the corner of a short length of sticky tape under the cord ...

... then roll it round the cord with your finger and thumb.

Sealing the cord end with a lighter.

You can also use a lighter. Place the end of the cord in the flame (do not apply the flame to the cord) for a fraction of a second, but no longer, or the end of the cord will become an ugly brown knob.

There is a new item on the market which does a good job of cutting and sealing synthetic cords all at once; it is called a thread zapper. It will cut thin cords very quickly, though thicker cords take longer, and it is a good way to avoid using a lighter. It is battery operated, heats up in seconds and cuts the cord cleanly. It is most useful at the end of a project when you need to cut the cord and seal it without spoiling the adjacent knot. It finishes the end neatly without the ugly dark knob which can result from using a lighter for too long.

The thread zapper in action.

Button and Braid Knots

These are two basic knots that you really need to learn. It would be very difficult to make a knotted necklace without the button knot, as it is such an elegant and useful knot for finishing and hiding the ends of the cords. The braid knot is a very quick way to embellish a necklace or bracelet using just a few beautiful beads.

Button knot necklace

This knot is best known as a Chinese button knot. However, its round shape is typical of Celtic style, and its endless cyclical design represents the eternal cycle of life in Celtic symbolism as well as in Chinese Buddhist symbolism. It is an incredibly useful knot for making jewellery. This necklace is finished with Keren's sliding knot, making the necklace adjustable and very versatile.

1. Seal the ends of the cords, place the bead in the middle of the cord and secure its position with pins.

2. On the right-hand side, thread on a small gold filler bead. Remove the pin.

3. Hold the bead and cord with your left hand and make a loop with your right hand.

4. Make another loop in front of the first one to create three spaces.

5. Insert the cord down into the first space on the right-hand side.

6. Bring the cord up through the centre hole.

Tying a button knot

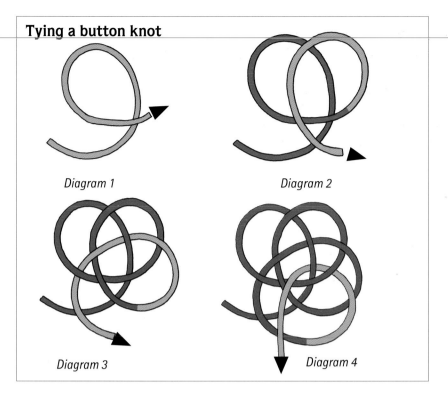

Diagram 1

Diagram 2

Diagram 3

Diagram 4

7. Insert the cord down again through the space on the left-hand side.

8. Pull the cord through but just enough to make a third loop on the right.

9. Bring the cord round to the right side and insert down into the new loop.

10. Bring it back up through the centre hole above your thumb.

11. Pull the cord through.

12. Pull the two ends gently to make the knot. Guide the knot towards the right side otherwise it becomes 'inside out'.

13. Pull the knot tight and pull the loops through one by one until they are flat against the knot.

14. The button knot should look like this.

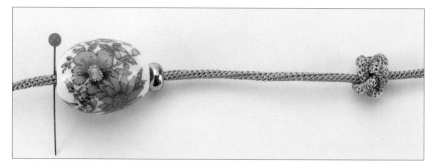

15. Button knots always end up about 10cm (4in) away from the position you want them in. Examine the cord between the bead and the knot and find which loop it becomes on the other side of the knot (see the diagram below).

16. Pull this loop until all the cord is pulled through the knot and it is next to the bead (see diagram).

17. Pull the next loop through in the same direction (see diagram 4). Continue until all eight loops have been tightened.

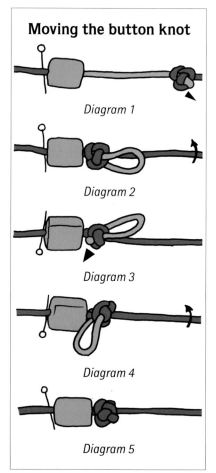

Moving the button knot

Diagram 1

Diagram 2

Diagram 3

Diagram 4

Diagram 5

18. Adjust the knot until you are happy with it; you will have to go round all the loops again to tighten the knot fully. There are no short cuts!

19. Add another gold bead on the other side of the knot, a blue glass bead and another gold bead.

20. Add gold beads, a button knot and a blue glass bead on the other side, so that the necklace is symmetrical.

21. Add a button knot, another blue glass bead flanked with gold beads and a button knot, then another blue bead with gold beads and a final button knot. Repeat this sequence on the other side. Thread on the closure about 10cm (4in) away from the knot.

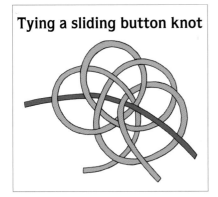

Tying a sliding button knot

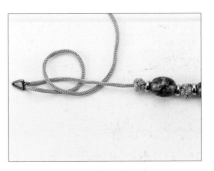

22. Take the end of the cord underneath itself.

23. Loop around in front of the cord and up behind it again.

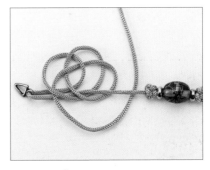

24. Loop around again in the same way and underneath the holding cord again. You are making a button knot in exactly the same way as pages 88–89 but looping it around the holding cord to create a sliding button knot. See the diagram above.

25. Thread the end of the cord into the first loop, up through the centre and down through the last loop.

26. Pull the cord through to make a third loop, then back to the right and underneath the cord again. Note that all the loops coming up are behind the holding cord and all those going down are in front of it.

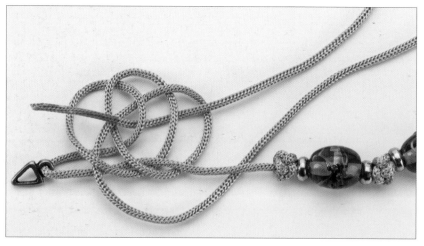

28. Tighten the knot, nudging it towards the right, otherwise the knot will be inside out.

27. Thread the cord down through the first loop and then up through the centre again.

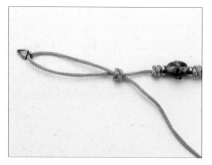

29. Your finished button knot should look like this. It will slide up to the left to make a longer necklace and to the right to make it shorter.

30. When you are satisfied that the length is correct (you may have to move the knot), trim off the end with the thread zapper or use scissors and a lighter to seal the end.

31. Repeat steps 21–30 with a hook closure, on the other side of the necklace (see the diagram below). Adjust the length of the sliding knot to match the other side.

Keren's sliding button knots used with a hook fastener. This knot was originally a mistake made by a student named Keren, which turned out to be incredibly useful.

Opposite

You can achieve many different looks using the simple button knot. All the necklaces shown have adjustable sliding knots, making them extremely versatile.

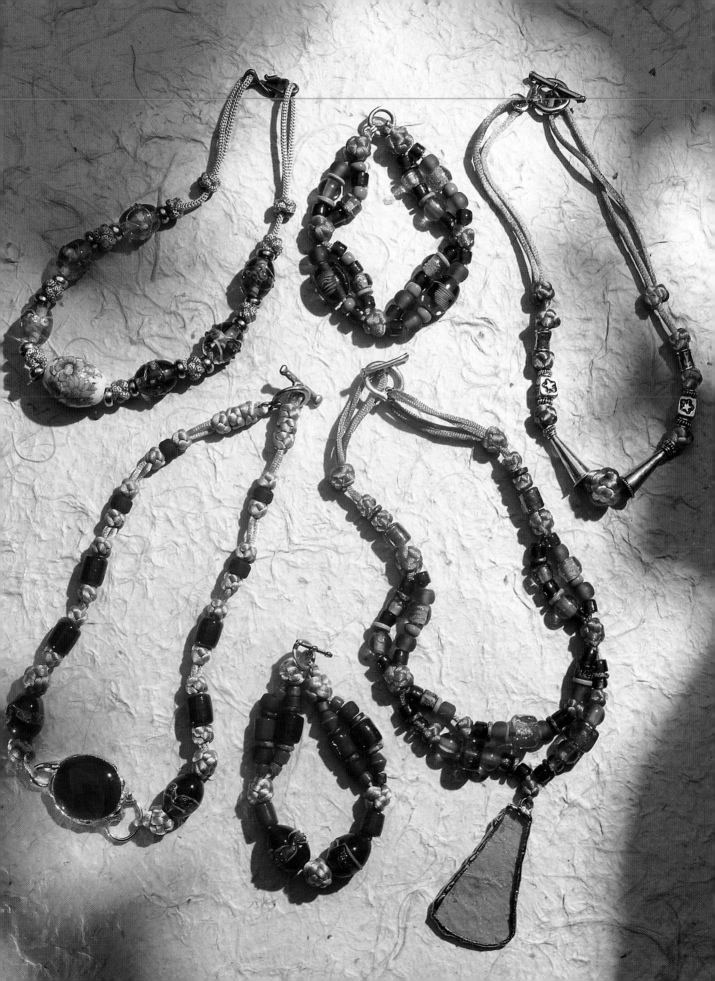

Braid knot necklace

The pattern of this knot is a basic pattern used frequently in Celtic design, and it is a quick and effective way to make a short, decorative, interwoven braid between beads and button knots. It is much more attractive and stable when the cords are doubled.

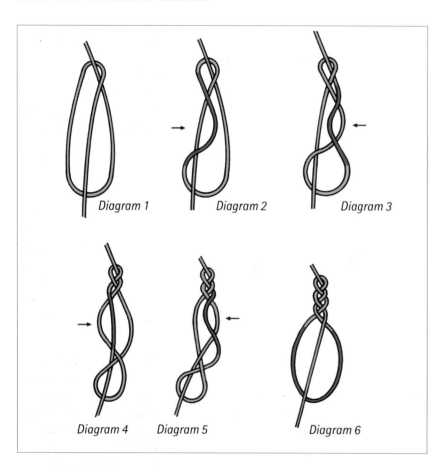

Diagram 1 *Diagram 2* *Diagram 3*

Diagram 4 *Diagram 5* *Diagram 6*

YOU WILL NEED

Two pieces of natural cotton cord, 3m (118in) each

Three large and two small painted wooden beads

Fourteen brass hexagonal nuts

Four brass flat washers

Brass hook and eye closure

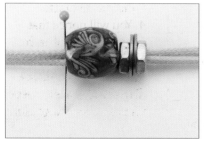

1. Thread two separate cords through a large wooden bead and secure the position with a pin. Thread a brass hexagonal nut, two brass washers and another brass nut on the right-hand side.

2. Use the doubled cord to make a button knot following the instructions on pages 88–89.

3. Tighten the knot partially. The cords should all be parallel, but you may find (as shown above) that they are not. If not, untwist them until they are parallel.

4. Loosen the knot and pull through the loops to move the knot closer to the bead, following the directions on page 90.

5. Your finished knot should look like this.

6. Add brass nuts, beads and button knots as above. Notice that the second and third button knots are smaller as only one cord was used to tie the knot around the other cord – see directions on page 91. Although this knot will not have the space to slide, it is tied in exactly the same way as a sliding button knot.

7. Pin the necklace into place on a cork mat and loop with two cords together around and under as shown.

8. Bring the cords down on the right and across to the middle; see diagram 1.

9. Start plaiting using the cords on the left-hand side, by bringing them into the middle – see diagram 2.

10. Take the cord on the right-hand side and bring it to the middle to continue the plait – see diagram 3. Continue plaiting by bringing the cords on the left to the middle as in diagram 4. You will notice that a mirror image of each crossing will form at the bottom of the knot (see diagram 5). These must be uncrossed as you go along.

11. Undo these unwanted crossings by pulling the cords out from the bottom loop and uncrossing the bottom loop as shown in diagram 6.

Tip

When using double cords to make the knot, if you start with the cords entering the knot on the left side, and finish with the cords emerging on the same (left) side, the two looped cords will fall neatly parallel. However, if you start with the cords entering the knot on the left side and finish with them emerging on the opposite (right) side, the looped cords will be twisted and will need to be untwisted throughout the knot.

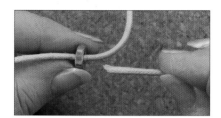

14. Make a button knot just after the plait, move it into position and thread on a brass nut. Thread one cord through the nut, then flatten it down to thread the other cord through.

12. When you come to the end of the plait, pull the cord through the loop at the bottom.

13. Ensure all the cords are parallel and flat. Tighten the plait.

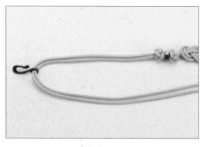

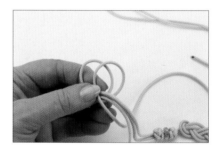

Tip

Alternate which piece of cord you use to make the button knots to ensure the lengths end up the same.

15. Make the next button knot with the longer cord. Thread on the fastener.

16. Make a button knot with one cord around the other three cords (instructions on page 91).

17. Use the longest cord to make another button knot around three cords and trim and seal the ends. Note that two sliding knots have been made side by side – with this thick cord, a double sliding button knot would have been too bulky.

18. Repeat steps 1–16 for the other side to finish the necklace. Ensure that both sides are the same length.

Button and braid necklaces in different styles, both elegant and rustic.

Plaits

Interlaced plaits were used as decoration by the ancient Egyptians, Greeks and Romans as well as the Celts. They are probably one of the most ancient designs in existence. Here you will learn how to make a three-stranded plait (also known as King Solomon's plait) and a four-stranded plait which results in a wider braid.

Three-stranded plait

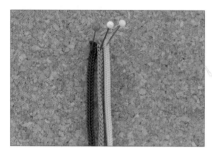

1. Start with three cords, all the same length.

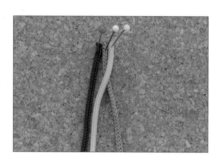

2. Take the right-hand-side cord over the middle cord so that it becomes the middle cord.

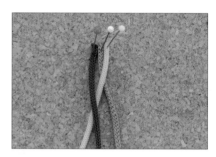

3. Take the left-hand-side cord into the middle.

4. Take the right-hand-side cord into the middle.

5. Take the left-hand side cord into the middle.

6. Take the right-hand-side cord into the middle.

7. Take the left-hand side cord into the middle.

8. Take the right-hand-side cord into the middle.

9. Continue until you have your desired length of plait.

Four-stranded plait

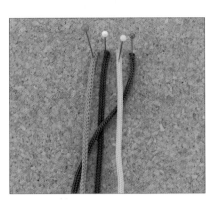

1. Start off with four cords, all of the same length.

2. Take the cord on the right-hand side underneath the next cord to the left, over the next cord and under the last cord on the far left.

3. Take the cord which is now on the far right (yellow here). Thread it under, then over, and then under the last cord on the left.

4. Take the cord which is now on the far right (deep red here). Thread it under, then over and under the cord on the far left-hand side.

5. Continue until you have your desired length of plait, straightening the plait to keep it vertical as you go along.

Plaited necklace with beads

This plait is an extended King Solomon's knot. It is said that all the wisdom of Solomon is contained in this knot, so the plait must contain even more wisdom! The addition of beads in several colours to complement the colour of the cord makes an interesting pattern when plaited. If you thread one third of the beads on to each strand before you start, it does not take very long to make the necklace.

YOU WILL NEED

2m (78in) 1mm (1/24in) cotton cord

1m (39in) 1mm (1/24in) cotton cord

Approximately 130 small glass beads

One larger bead for the closure

1. Fold the 2m (78in) cord in half to make a loop. With one end of the 1m length, make two button knots around the folded 2m cord to create the loop at the end. The longer piece of the 1m (39in) piece of cord makes the third strand of the necklace. Cut off the short end and add a dab of instant glue gel to secure it.

2. Pin the necklace into place and add one third of the beads on to each cord. Leave them on the ends to slide up when needed.

3. Slide each bead up into place before making each crossover. Refer to page 98 if you are unsure of the plaiting method.

4. Continue until the desired length is achieved.

5. Thread the large bead on to two of the cords, bring the ends around and use one of them to make a button knot around the other three (folded) cords and the remaining cord. Tighten the knot and trim the ends. Add a spot of instant glue gel to secure the ends.

You can use a variety of beads to create different effects for your jewellery.

Turk's Head Knots

This is a very ancient and elegant knot. The continuous pattern of the Turk's head knot was regarded by the Christian Celts as a symbol of connection and continuity for eternity. Its name is believed to have originated from the similarity between this knot and a turban.

Turk's head bangle

The bangle is made with one single cord which is woven around a cylinder to make nine circuits; three to make the basic plait and six more circuits to treble the plait. It is continuous and the join is invisible on the outside. The knot is constructed around a cardboard cylinder about 7cm (2¾in) in diameter. A larger cylinder may be needed depending on the wrist size. You are actually making a three-stranded plait (see page 98) but because the cord is continuous, you make it with one cord at a time instead of three. This bangle has three circuits of the cord plaited over and under each other eleven times to make a total of eleven 'scallops' or curves on each side. Generally the number of 'crossovers' depends on the size of the cylinder you are working around. To make the steps clearer here, the knot has been made around a glass so that you can see the back of the knot as well as the front.

YOU WILL NEED

3m (118in) 2mm (1/12in) braided macramé cord

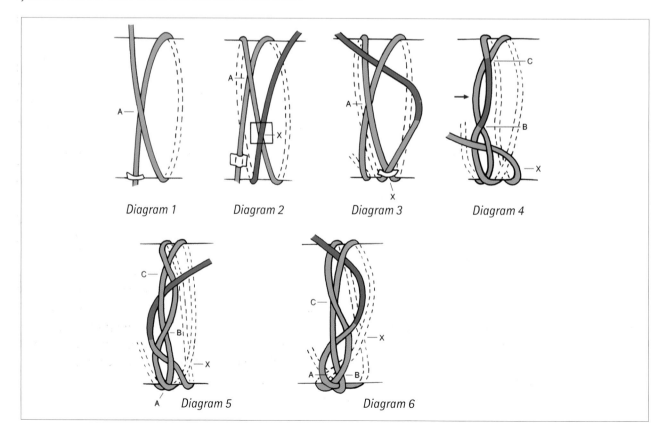

Diagram 1   Diagram 2   Diagram 3   Diagram 4

Diagram 5   Diagram 6

1. Imagine that the glass in the photograph is a cardboard cylinder. Stiffen the mobile end of the cord (see page 87). Tape the fixed end of the cord to the left side of the cylinder and make one rotation of the cord, crossing at point A (see diagram 1).

2. Make another rotation of the cord and bring it round to the front in between the two cords already there, crossing over the right-hand cord at point X (see diagram 2). Anchor this crossing temporarily using sticky tape (see bottom of diagram 3) as it tends to uncross during plaiting later on.

3. Thread the cord underneath the top cord on the right-hand side, as in diagram 3.

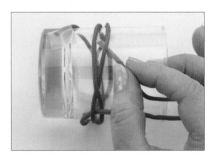

4. Pull the cord through, in between the two cords. Rotate the cylinder towards you, then cross the left-hand fixed cord over the right-hand one (see diagram 4). The new crossing points are shown as B and C.

5. Take the end of the mobile cord and thread it underneath the left-hand cord and over the right-hand cord between B and C (see diagram 5). You can see that the plait is beginning to take shape.

6. Rotate the cylinder slightly towards you, and above crossing C, thread the mobile end under the right-hand cord (see diagram 6).

7. Repeat step 4.

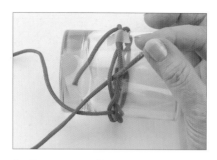

8. Repeat step 5.

9. The cord goes over the right-hand side then above the crossing and underneath the right-hand-side cord, as in step 6. Repeat steps 4, 5 and 6 until the desired number of scallops is reached.

Tip

If your cylinder is larger you may need more crossings, but do not make the first plait too tight as you have to double and treble it.

10. By now, you should have reached your starting point. Follow the path through again to make the plait double.

11. Continue following the cord through until you reach the starting point again. Follow the path around again so that the plait is trebled.

12. Bring the cord ends to the inside and trim the ends off, leaving about 1cm (½in) to be glued down.

13. Seal the ends with a thread zapper or a lighter and secure with instant glue gel. Coat the bangle with diluted PVA glue to keep the shape (see page 84).

You can make your bangle in any colour you wish.

Figure-of-eight Chains

The figure-of-eight pattern is one of the twelve elementary Celtic knots. Although one knot is not self-contained in the same way as the triangular knot or the circle-of-life knot, a chain of figures of eight is made from one continuous line which is also a symbol of eternity – a positive, life-affirming theme in Celtic knotwork. To the Irish scribes of the seventh to ninth centuries, the endless line represented the boundlessness of God.

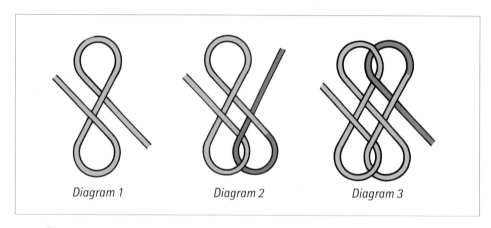

Diagram 1   *Diagram 2*   *Diagram 3*

1. Make a figure of eight and pin it in place. Follow the 'overs and unders' shown, as in diagram 1.

2. Loop around to start the next figure of eight and link into the bottom of the first figure of eight (see diagram 2).

3. Loop around to make the top of the eight and link to the top of the previous figure of eight (see diagram 3).

4. Continue making the figures of eight, linking each one into the previous one.

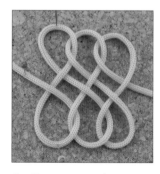

5. Carry on until you have achieved the desired length of chain.

Figure-of-eight chain bangle

Some say intertwining knots represent the interconnectedness of all life. Others say that they can be devices to bind negativity – it becomes entangled in the knot and cannot escape. Whatever you like to believe, this chain makes a very attractive bangle and is easy to make.

YOU WILL NEED

3m (118in) 2mm (1/12in) cord in turquoise

3m (118in) 2mm (1/12in) cord in purple

1. Start a figure-of-eight chain on a cork mat and work about seventeen or eighteen loops.

Tip

The method is shown with only one cord to make the steps easier to follow. To make the bracelet with two colours, weave the second colour in as shown above after step 1.

2. Make a cylinder with a sheet of A4 paper, and secure your chain on to it.

3. Thread the end of the cord on the left-hand side under and through the bottom loop on the right-hand side.

4. Thread it underneath the bottom loop on the left-hand side.

5. Take the end of the cord underneath to make the bottom loop of the figure of eight.

6. The cord then passes over the other end of the cord, under the next loop and over to pass back again.

7. The cord then goes over and under the loop on the left-hand side.

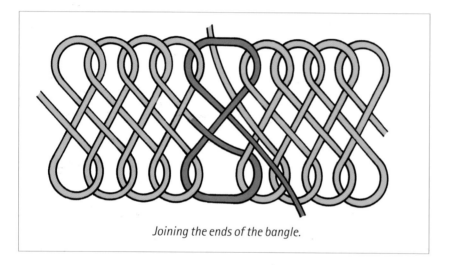

Joining the ends of the bangle.

8. Take the cord under the middle of the figure of eight. Trim and seal the ends using a lighter or thread zapper, and secure them on the inside with instant glue gel as in steps 12 and 13 on page 104. Apply PVA glue to the bangle so that it retains its shape.

Opposite
Use various coloured cords to achieve the effect you want.

Horizontal figure-of-eight chain

The figure of eight is not so easily recognisable when laid on its side, however, its flowing curves make a very attractive and intricate chain.

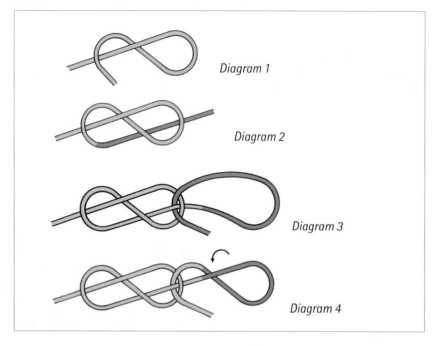

Diagram 1

Diagram 2

Diagram 3

Diagram 4

1. Start the chain with a figure of eight on its side.

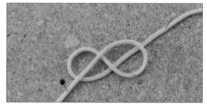

2. Take the cord up and underneath the 'eight' towards the top right-hand corner.

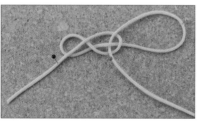

3. Loop around and over, then under and over again.

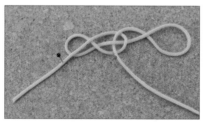

4. Turn the large loop over to form a figure of eight.

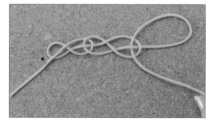

5. Repeat steps 2 and 3, taking the cord end under the loop on the right, then loop back again and then over, under and over again.

6. Repeat steps 4 and 5. When you are satisfied that the chain is the length you want, tuck the free straight cords at the beginning and end through the last loops, as shown in the diagrams.

Horizontal figure-of-eight chain necklace

This horizontal figure-of-eight chain works up very quickly. Here, no beads have been added, but a pendant could look very nice with it, as you can see on page 113.

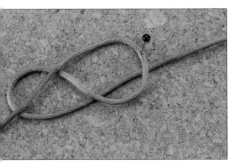

1. Form the first figure of eight using the turquoise cord, leaving enough cord at the end for a button knot and closures on the left-hand side.

You will need

3m (118in) 2mm ($\frac{1}{12}$in) cord in a natural beige colour

3m (118in) 2mm ($\frac{1}{12}$in) cord in turquoise

3m (118in) 2mm ($\frac{1}{12}$in) cord in deep blue

Brass ring and toggle closure

2. Loop backwards over the cord, then under and over again as in step 3 on page 110.

Tip

The necklace can be as short or as long as you want. Keep adding knots until you are happy with the length.

3. Following step 4 on page 110, turn the large loop over and repeat steps 2 and 3. Keep building up the chain, adding knots to form the necklace.

4. Add the natural beige cord, leaving a short end at the beginning. This will be threaded through the closure and woven back through the button knot. Follow the path of the turquoise cord, keeping the cords side-by-side. Work the second cord through the length of the necklace.

5. Add in the deep blue cord. Start at the beginning, leaving a long end (this will form the button knot over the turquoise cord). Work the third cord through to the end of the chain.

Tip
The three cord ends will need securing with tape as you move the chain off the cork base. Remove the tape before moving on to step 6.

6. Tuck the free straight cords at the beginning and end of the chain through the last loops. Pass the two blue cords at both ends through the closures after trimming and sealing the beige cord neatly to hide it between the blue cords. Form button knots by working the deep blue cord around the other cords (see page 91). After the button knots are tightened and moved up into the correct place in the design, the ends of the blue cords should be trimmed and sealed neatly.

Opposite

The finished necklace and another example with a pendant. The pendant is secured by weaving the gold cord into the pattern of the necklace, enhancing the design.

Interlaced Knots

Celtic interlacing is almost endless in its variations; it can go in any direction as long as it follows the traditional Celtic knotwork principle of alternate 'overs and unders'.

Celtic cross

This cross is made with two different coloured cords, the tan colour starts at the top of the design and the rust coloured cord starts at the bottom of the cross and becomes part of the necklace.

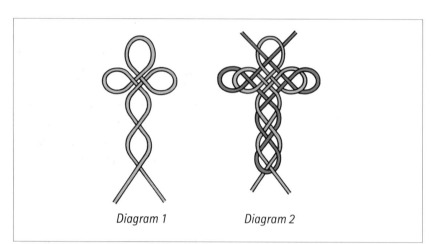

Diagram 1   *Diagram 2*

YOU WILL NEED

2m (78in) 1mm (¹⁄₂₄in) nylon cord in a rust colour

1m (39in) 1mm (¹⁄₂₄in) nylon cord in a tan colour

Two gold Celtic torpedo beads

Brass-coloured hook and eye closure

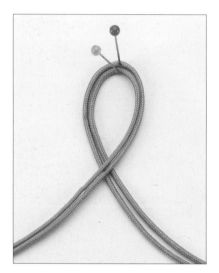

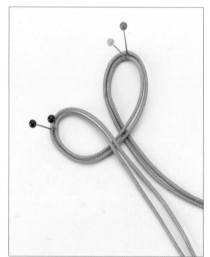

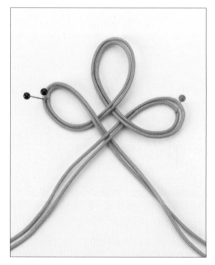

1. Fold the shorter tan piece of cord in half, then fold in half again to make the loop at the top. Pin it in place.

2. Make a loop on the left-hand side and pin it in place. Follow the overs and unders in diagram 1 carefully.

3. Make another loop on the right-hand side and pin it in place.

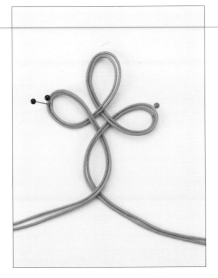

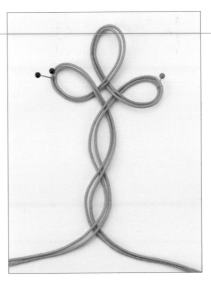

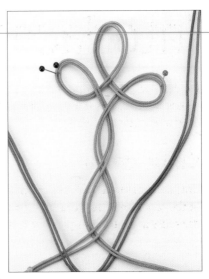

4. Make a loop in the middle, laying the cords on the right-hand side over the cords from the left.

5. Make another loop, again laying the cords from the right-hand side over the cords from the left.

6. Take the rust cord, fold it in half twice as before and pin it into place as shown, starting at the bottom of the cross pattern. The right-hand-side rust cords go under the tan cords and the left-hand side rust cords go over the tan cords.

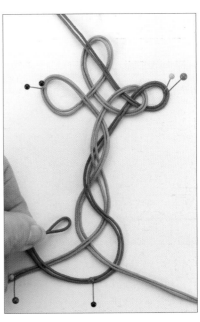

7. Take the right-hand-side cords over the cross and then under it.

8. Make a loop with the rust cords, pin it in place and thread it under the tan-coloured loop on the right-hand side, following diagram 2.

9. Take the rust cords over themselves then under the top of the right-hand-side loop. Continue over the top loop as shown.

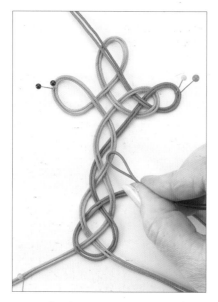

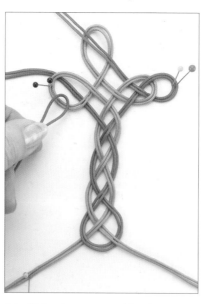

10. Take the rust cords on the left-hand side under the tan cord, over the rust cord and under the tan cord on the right-hand side.

11. Take the rust cord back over the tan cord, under itself, over the tan cord again on the left and under the loop on the left-hand side.

12. Repeat steps 8 and 9 to make the rust loop on the left-hand side. Continue up under the tan loop at the top and over the rust cord, following diagram 2 throughout.

13. Unpin the cross and tighten it. The long rust cords are used to make the rest of the necklace. Trim and secure the tan cords.

14. Add button knots, the gold beads and the closures and secure with sliding double button knots as before.

The finished necklace.

Try different coloured leather cords and beads to create a variety of beautiful cross necklaces.

Triangular knot earrings

This knot is also known as a Triquetra, a Celtic symbol of the Triple Goddess. The triple sign was a common symbol in Celtic myth and legend and the idea of three in one is a possible reason why Christian beliefs such as that of the Trinity were so easily adopted by the Celtic people. The sign represented the three domains of the earth, sea and sky, the trinity of mind, body and soul and many other triple concepts as well.

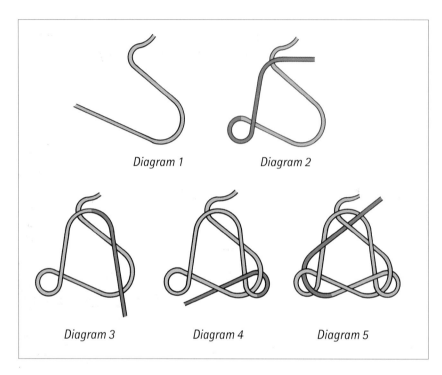

Diagram 1

Diagram 2

Diagram 3

Diagram 4

Diagram 5

YOU WILL NEED

Two pieces of 1mm (1/24in) leather cord each 50cm (20in) long

Two earring hooks

1. Thread the earring hook on to the cord to about half way and secure it with pins. Make an S-shaped loop as in diagram 1 and pin it in place.

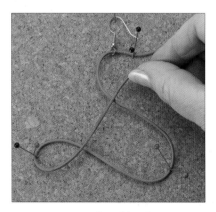

2. Loop around and back up to the top, as in diagram 2.

3. Pin the shape in place.

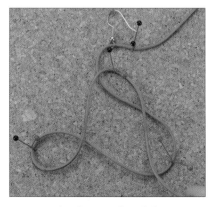

4. Loop back round and down, as in diagram 3.

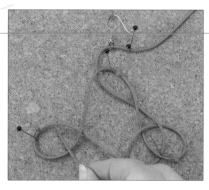

5. Loop around the outside edge, underneath the outside and over the centre and under the bottom cord, as in diagram 4.

6. Thread the cord through the loop on the left-hand side as shown.

7. Bring the cord back over, near the top of the earring.

8. Then under and over again on the right-hand side, as in diagram 5.

9. Go back round to the left and follow the path of the cord again to make the knot double thickness. Trim and secure the ends as shown on page 104.

Finished triangular knot earrings, incorporating the Celtic symbol of the Triple Goddess.

Two heart brooch

The heart shape is universally considered to be an expression of love. It is a relatively new symbol and would not have been in use in the time of the early Christian Celts. However, its inclusion in the vocabulary of symbolic knotwork shows that Celtic artwork is a living and evolving tradition.

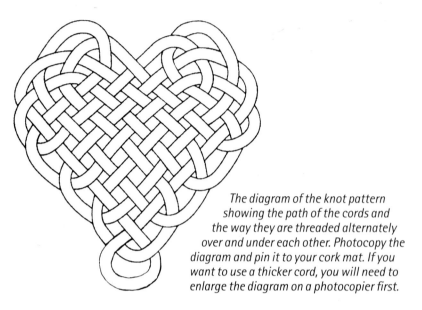

The diagram of the knot pattern showing the path of the cords and the way they are threaded alternately over and under each other. Photocopy the diagram and pin it to your cork mat. If you want to use a thicker cord, you will need to enlarge the diagram on a photocopier first.

YOU WILL NEED

1.5m (59in) 1mm (¹⁄₂₄in) nylon cord in dark red

Three pieces of 1mm (¹⁄₂₄in) pink nylon cord, each 1.5m (59in) long

Brooch bar

Small piece of thin leather same size as brooch bar

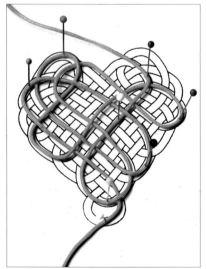

1. Find the middle of the cord and pin it to the centre of the bottom loop on the diagram. Following the guide lines, pin the right half of the cord over or under the crossings as shown on the diagram. Continue until the top of the heart is reached.

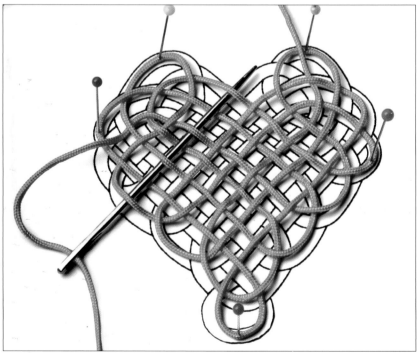

2. Weave the left side of the cord through with a smooth-tipped tapestry needle, following the diagram.

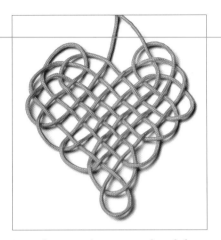

3. When you have completed the heart with one cord, unpin it. Any mistakes will be apparent, as the cord will spring up.

4. Weave in the second cord, following the lead of the first cord, starting at the bottom and using the tapestry needle as before.

5. Tighten all the cords as shown above. Make another heart knot using only pink cord and following the steps shown above.

6. Trim and secure the end of the cords neatly using instant glue gel. Glue the brooch pin to a small piece of thin leather and then stick this on to the two-tone heart with instant glue gel. Attach the pink heart to the first heart using small spots of instant glue gel.

You can use the heart knot to make a variety of jewellery.

Josephine knot necklace

This is an ancient Celtic knot that has been popular for thousands of years. It can be found in various cultures, each of which has a different name for the knot. Josephine is a relatively recent name, after Napoleon Bonaparte's Empress. Since there is ample evidence that early Celtic society was matriarchal, it is appropriate to use the name here. In this necklace the knots are linked from side to side and made using just one continuous cord – an unusual style and very attractive. The beaded scallops stabilise the necklace design.

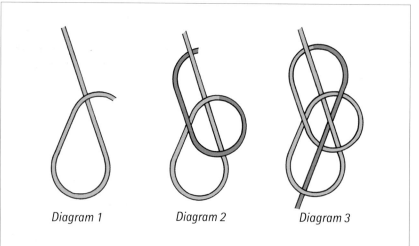

Diagram 1   *Diagram 2*   *Diagram 3*

YOU WILL NEED

4m (160in) 2mm (1/12in) black cotton cord

1.5m (59in) 1mm (1/24in) black cotton cord

130 assorted colour glass beads

Hook and eye closure

1. Make a loop with the 2mm (1/12in) cotton cord (see diagram 1) and pin it in place.

2. Make another loop on top, and slightly to the right (see diagram 2).

3. Cross the cord over and then under as shown.

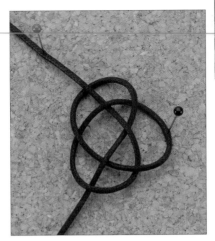

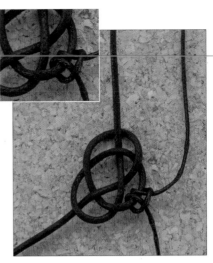

4. Loop around and over, then under, over and under.

5. Pull the cord through so the knot takes shape as above (see diagram 3). Repeat steps 1–5 to make another knot below the first one. Continue until you have made about twelve knots.

6. Take the length of thinner cord and tie a larkshead knot (shown above) to the top Josephine knot in the necklace.

7. Add about nine beads to the short end of the thin cord and pin it in place as shown.

8. Add about eleven beads to the next scallop and loop through the next Josephine knot as shown to begin another larkshead knot.

9. Loop the thinner cord through the Josephine knot again.

10. Bring the cord underneath the loop to finish the larkshead knot. Continue until you have added beaded scallops to each Josephine knot, adding eleven beads each time.

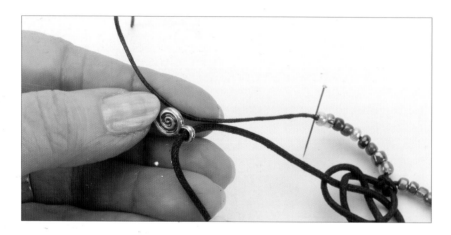

11. Add nine beads to the end of the thinner cord after the last larkshead knot. Secure them with a pin as shown. Thread the closure on to the thicker piece of cord.

12. With the end of the thicker cord, make a button knot around the thin cord and the two cords to secure. Tighten the button knot, then cut and secure the thin cord with instant glue gel to stop it slipping out.

13. Repeat steps 11 and 12 for the other end of the necklace, using the hook fastener instead of the eye.

Jospehine knots create intricate patterns, perfect for necklaces and bracelets. The necklace and bracelet in black and the blue necklace with the turquoise pendant were also made with Josephine knots, but the series of knots was made in the more traditional vertical style, starting with the cord folded in half, and the knots made with the two cord ends, one on each side.

Celtic square knot necklace

To the monks of early Christianity, the square symbolised the creation of the manifold universe. They used the geometric method of construction to create knots to fill squares in their designs for embellishing manuscripts. This knot fits into a square, although here it has been adapted it to make a necklace with a pendant so the shape has become slightly elongated. Knots made with cord (compared to knots constructed geometrically on paper) have a life of their own!

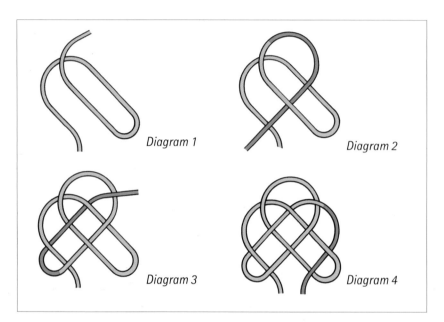

Diagram 1

Diagram 2

Diagram 3

Diagram 4

YOU WILL NEED

3m (118in) silver coloured 2mm (¹⁄₁₂in) satin cord

3m (118in) turquoise 2mm (¹⁄₁₂in) braided cord

One Celtic silver circular pendant

Two Celtic spangle hexagonal silver beads

Six Celtic oval silver beads

1. Find the middle of the silver cord and fold the cord in half at this point. Tie a larkshead knot around the Celtic pendant.

2. Make a loop with the cord on the left-hand side (see diagram 1).

3. Take the right-hand-side cord and thread it over, under and over the other cord (see diagram 2).

4. Loop the cord around, taking it up and under, over then under (see diagram 3).

5. Loop the cord around the top, take it under and then over, following diagram 4. Tidy the knot, making sure it is symmetrical.

6. Find the middle of the turquoise cord, pin it in place as shown and start to follow the path of the silver cord around again.

7. Finish following the path of the first knot with the turquoise cord.

8. Make a button knot with the silver cord around the other three cords. Then make two button knots further down with the turquoise cord.

9. Continue adding beads and knots as shown.

10. Finish with two sliding double button knots.

The finished necklace.

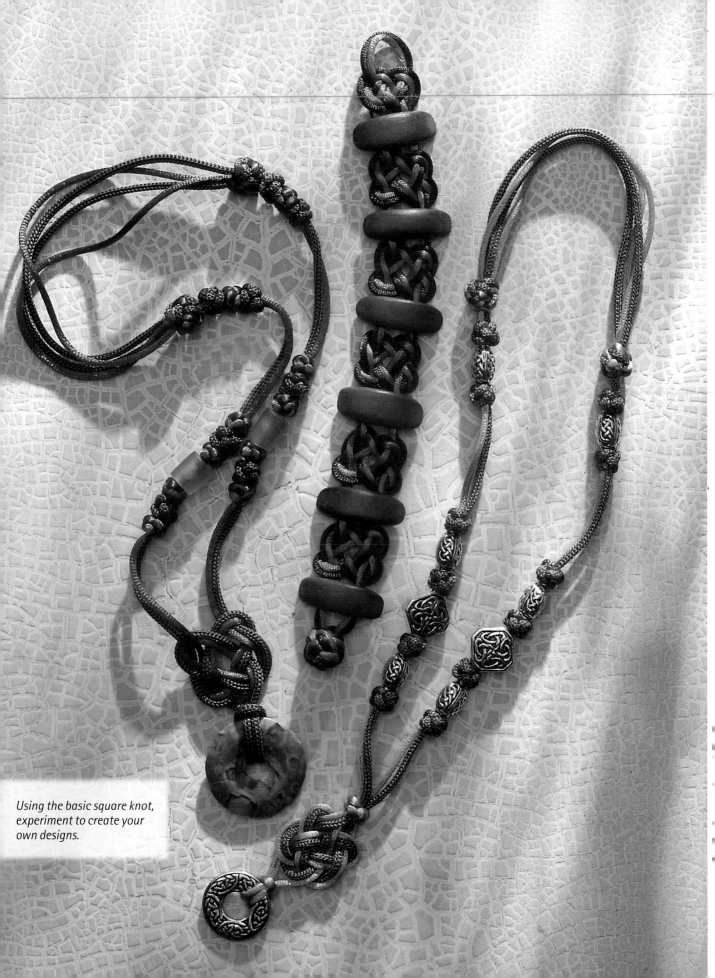

Using the basic square knot, experiment to create your own designs.

Glass Painting

Craftsmen discovered the magic of painting art in the first century AD, and since then coloured glass has been used to decorate churches, cathedrals and homes. Originally, glass-painted vessels had to be fired to permanently fix the colours to the surface, but nowadays we have access to a whole range of air-drying paints that do not require firing in a kiln.

These new paints enable us to emulate classic techniques very easily. The vibrant colours can be blended together, and even textured and frosted effects can be achieved simply. Glass painting outliners are also readily available, and these can be used to reproduce the classic leaded effect in stained-glass work. Self-adhesive lead is a relatively new product on the market, and this gives an even more realistic, antique finish to a glass-painted panel or window.

Celtic art is breathtaking, and in this chapter original Celtic designs have been simplified and adapted for glass painting whilst retaining, it is hoped, the energy and power of the original patterns and motifs. Spirals, knotwork and zoomorphic designs are included, as well as figures and initials – all painted in glorious rich colours, and in some cases either gilded or embellished.

Opposite

Angel panel

You can include many glass painting and embellishment techniques on one piece of glass. This panel combines lead, outliner, painting, gilding, and embellishment with coloured stones and dots of gold outliner.

Materials and Equipment

Outliners, self-adhesive lead, glass paints and gilding products are available from all good art and craft outlets, and you should be able to find the rest of the materials in your own home. Because of the intricacy of Celtic design, you will have to choose your glass items carefully. The main thing to remember is to keep them simple. Clip frames are ideal as they are inexpensive and available in a variety of sizes. Simple, chunky vases, goblets and bottles can be found in junk shops, DIY and kitchen outlets, supermarkets and gift shops.

Outliners

Designs need to be outlined first before they can be painted and there are various outliners available which are specifically designed for painting on glass.

1 Draughting film ink This is used with a technical pen for drawing on a smooth surface.

2 Technical pen You can outline or draw fine detail with this.

3 Black outliner You can apply raised lines with this.

4 Metallic outliner This is used to create raised outlines and decoration on painted pieces.

5 Boning tool This is used to rub down self-adhesive lead.

6 Self-adhesive lead Different widths are available. This can be used for simple designs and borders.

Glass paints

Water-based and solvent-based glass paints are available from art and craft outlets. They are transparent and manufactured specifically for application to glass and other smooth surfaces. The majority of these paints are purely decorative and not intended for functional items, therefore care has to be taken when finished items are washed. Some water-based glass paints and outliners can be baked in a domestic oven, which makes them both durable and dishwasher safe. Always check the manufacturers' instructions carefully.

The paints are available in a wide variety of rich, vibrant colours and are intermixable within their range. However, solvent-based paints will not mix with water-based paints. Do not shake the bottles before you use them, as this

will create air bubbles. Apply them liberally straight from the bottle to achieve a smooth stained-glass effect, then allow them to settle flat. Always make sure that your painted pieces are left to dry in a dust-free area, or cover them carefully with an upturned box.

Peel-off paints are transparent, water-based paints supplied in bottles fitted with fine nozzles. They can be used to decorate glass, mirrors, ceramic ware and porcelain. They are available in a wide variety of colours and metallic effects, and include an outliner range.

Other materials

You will not need all the items shown here when you start glass painting. The projects show exactly what you will need to complete each design.

Cutting mat Cut self-adhesive lead on a cutting mat.

Masking tape Used to secure patterns to glass before outlining.

Ceramic paint This is painted or sponged on to the back of glass to give a flat finish when viewed from the front.

Oil paint Burnt umber is used to age a gilded surface.

Synthetic round paintbrushes You will need Nos. 2 and 4 to apply the paint.

Large soft brush Used to brush away any loose leaf when gilding.

Palette Used for mixing colours.

Pieces of sponge Synthetic sponges are great for applying paint.

White spirit Clean brushes used with solvent-based paint with this.

Methylated spirits Used to clean glass.

Strong clear glue Attach glass droplets to glass with this.

Water Clean brushes used with water-based paint with this.

Spray glue Used to attach a paper pattern to a glass surface.

Shellac A coat will protect a gilded piece of work.

Dutch metal leaf Used for gilding. wIt is available in sheets with various metallic finishes.

Gilding size Used as an adhesive for Dutch metal leaf.

Scissors Cut out patterns with these.

Scalpel You should cut self-adhesive lead with this.

White paper Used as a backing when painting designs.

Parchment paper This can replace the backing sheet of a clip frame to give a more authentic look.

Absorbent paper Wipe nozzles and brushes, and mop up spills with this. It can also be used with methylated spirits to clean surfaces.

Cotton buds Wipe away outliner mistakes and correct small paint spills with these.

Glass droplets You can add decoration with these.

Blanks There are many blank items available that you can decorate – clip frames, goblets, plates and more.

Plastic pockets These are used as a base when working with peel-off paints.

Technical pen Outline or draw fine detail with this.

Draughting film ink Use this with the technical pen for drawing on a smooth surface.

Boning tool Used for smoothing and flattening self-adhesive lead on to glass.

Celtic Corners

This project introduces you to peel-off paint, which is great fun to use. The designs are outlined then filled in with paint. When dry, they can be peeled off and applied to glass, metal and ceramics, on two- and three-dimensional surfaces. The paint is applied straight from the bottle and designs take approximately twenty-four hours to dry. The colours are milky at first, but they become transparent when dry. It is advisable not to peel them off before they are completely dry, or they may tear.

Corner pattern
Enlarge on a photocopier to the required size.

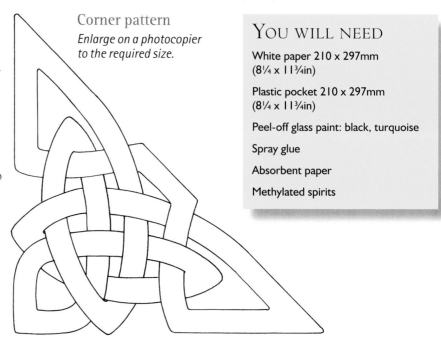

YOU WILL NEED

White paper 210 x 297mm (8¼ x 11¾in)

Plastic pocket 210 x 297mm (8¼ x 11¾in)

Peel-off glass paint: black, turquoise

Spray glue

Absorbent paper

Methylated spirits

1. Photocopy the design four times. Cut each one out, then glue all four on to a sheet of white paper.

2. Slip the paper into a plastic pocket and smooth it flat to remove any trapped air. Using black, start at the top and outline each design. Keep wiping the tip of the nozzle with absorbent paper to prevent clogging. Also, make sure there are no gaps, or the design might tear when you remove it from the plastic pocket.

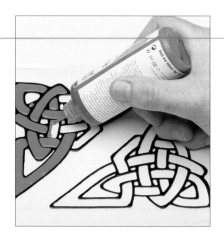  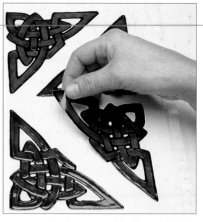

3. Use turquoise and carefully flood colour into the knotwork. Make sure that you fill in all the sections so there are no gaps. If air bubbles appear in the paint, prick them with a pin.

4. Fill in all the sections behind the knotwork with clear paint. This appears white when wet, but will become transparent as it dries.

5. Finish painting the four designs. Leave to dry for twenty-four hours, then carefully peel each one away from the plastic pocket.

Tip

Do not try to peel the designs away from the plastic pocket before they are completely dry, as they may tear – and do not apply them to a window or mirror if the surface is very warm or cold, as they may distort or break.
The designs may lose adhesion if they are moved several times. Just dampen the reverse sides with water and they will stick to the surface.

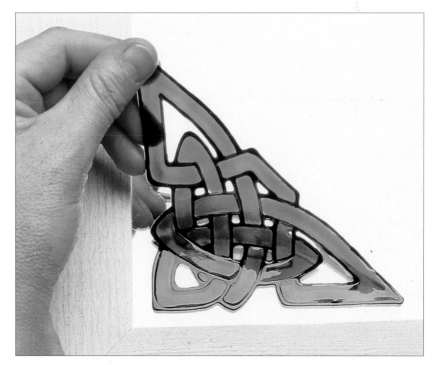

6. Clean the surface of a mirror or window with methylated spirits to remove any grease, then place one design in each corner. Press them on to the surface firmly.

Opposite

Knotwork vase

Motifs using peel-off paint can be applied to three-dimensional surfaces such as vases, bottles, jars and candlesticks. Use the techniques shown on the previous pages to create your own designs. Here, the central glass droplet is placed on the wet paint, and this acts as a glue when dry.

Pattern for the knotwork vase opposite.

Pattern for the Celtic chalice on page 138.

Pattern for the gilded bowl on page 139.

Above

Gilded bowl

Photocopy and enlarge the pattern several times. Join the pieces together with masking tape to form a strip that will fit inside your bowl, then outline and paint the design. Gild the inside and seal it with clear varnish.

Opposite

Celtic chalice

With a little outliner and paint you can transform a plain glass goblet into a beautiful Celtic chalice. Enlarge and photocopy the pattern enough times to form a continuous strip that will fit around the rim.

Patterns for the knotwork designs opposite.

Knotwork designs.

Decorative Plate

A technical pen is used in this project. With its fine nib you can achieve beautifully detailed work, which would be difficult with an outliner. The design is drawn on to the back of a glass plate, then opaque ceramic paints are used to block in the design. The surface is then sponged, thus sealing in the fine pen work. When the plate is viewed from the front, it has a truly professional appearance. This design has a vitality which is enhanced by the choice of gold against a dark background. The dogs chase each other around a central motif in a never-ending dance, full of life and energy.

YOU WILL NEED

Glass plate

White paper

Technical pen, fitted with a 0.5mm nib

Draughting film ink

Self-adhesive lead 3mm (⅛in) wide

Boning tool

Solvent-based ceramic paints: gold, dark blue

No. 2 paintbrush

Newspaper

Pieces of sponge

Palette

Cutting mat and scalpel

Spray glue

Absorbent paper

Methylated spirits

Pattern for the decorative plate

Increase or decrease the size on a photocopier so that it will fit comfortably within the flat base of your plate. All the work is done on the back of the plate, so this design will be reversed when viewed from the front.

1. Lightly spray the front of the pattern with glue, then press it face down on to the centre of the plate.

Tip

Always clean a glass surface with methylated spirits before working with a technical pen, so that the ink adheres to the surface. It is easy to remove mistakes using a damp cotton bud.

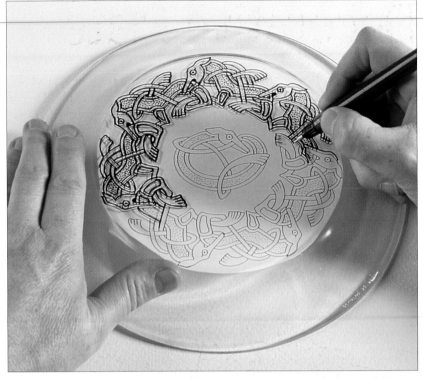

2. Turn the plate over and wipe the surface with methylated spirits. Outline the border with a technical pen. Leave to dry. Outline the central motif. Leave to dry.

3. Replace the pattern with a circle of white paper. Using a No. 2 paintbrush and gold paint, work on the back of the plate and paint the central motif. Apply the colour generously and carefully work round the border, filling it all in. Leave to dry for twenty-four hours.

4. Remove the white paper. Lay a sheet of newspaper over the work surface to protect it. Place the plate on a roll of tape to lift it up slightly, then pour dark blue paint into a palette and sponge it on to the back of the plate. This will create air bubbles but these will disperse. Leave to dry for twenty-four hours, then sponge on another coat of dark blue.

5. Turn the plate over and measure a strip of lead slightly larger than the circumference. Cut it, pull off the backing and stick it around the edge, leaving a slight overlap at the join.

6. Rub the lead flat with the boning tool, working round the edge of the plate with smooth movements until you meet the overlap.

7. Cut through both of the thicknesses in the centre of the overlapping section.

8. Remove the end of the overlapping top section and discard it.

9. Carefully peel back the rest of the top overlap. Remove the bottom section.

10. Butt the two ends together and rub the ends smooth with the boning tool.

Decorative plate

This plate is backpainted, which creates a beautifully flat finish when viewed from the front. The energy of the zoomorphic design is captured in the brilliance of the gold, as the dogs ceaselessly chase each other against the opaque blue background.

Pattern for the red and gold plate opposite.
All the work is done on the back of the plate, so the design will be
reversed when viewed from the front.

Red and gold plate

The inspiration for this design is taken from the symbol for St Luke – the calf as
represented in the Book of Kells. It is possible to achieve the fine detailing on the
wings and body if you use a technical pen.

Patterns for the zoomorphic designs opposite.

Zoomorphic designs.

Window Panel

Glass paint runs, so in order to paint a vertical window panel you need to work on a flat glass panel and then fix the design to the window with self-adhesive lead – an easy answer to a difficult problem. Also, if you move house, simply remove the lead and take the panel with you!

In the pattern opposite, the thicker lines show you where to place the self-adhesive lead. Glass can be cut to size at a glaziers. Make sure that the panel fits comfortably within your existing window.

YOU WILL NEED

Circular 2mm (1/12in) glass panel with smoothed edges, 34cm (13 1/2in) diameter

Masking tape

Self-adhesive lead: 3mm (1/8in) wide double-ribbed, and 9mm (3/8in) wide flat

Boning tool

Black outliner

Technical pen, fitted with a 0.5mm nib

Draughting film ink

White paper

Solvent-based paints: yellow, orange, blue, green, red, clear

No. 4 paintbrush

Cutting mat

Scalpel

Absorbent paper

Methylated spirits

Strong clear glue

3 small blue glass droplets

1 large blue glass droplet

1. Place the glass panel on top of the pattern. Use small pieces of masking tape to secure the edges. Clean the surface with methylated spirits.

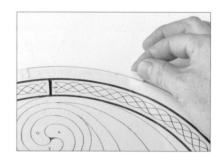

2. Cut a 7cm (2 3/4in) length of 3mm (1/8in) lead. Cut down the centre rib and remove the backing paper from one length. Press the strip on to the glass over one of the three outer spokes. Cut to fit. Repeat twice more on the remaining spokes.

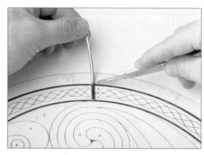

3. Cut a 100cm (39 1/4in) length of 3mm (1/8in) lead. Cut it down the centre with a scalpel and remove the paper backing from one strip. Place it round the outer circle. Trim the other strip to 90cm (35 1/2in) and remove the backing. Press it round the inner circle.

Pattern for the window panel

*Enlarge on a photocopier to
fit your window.*

1 *Yellow*

2 *Orange*

3 *Amber – mix equal quantities of orange and yellow*

4 *Blue*

5 *Green*

6 *Light green – mix clear paint with a little green*

7 *Red*

4. Rub the lead borders and spokes firmly down on to the glass with the boning tool. Trim the ends.

5. Run the tip of the boning tool round all the edges to seal the lead to the glass.

6. Use black outliner to outline the central spiral, then the three outer spirals and leaves. If blobs form on the end of the nozzle, wipe them away with absorbent paper and continue working. Leave to dry for thirty minutes.

7. Clean the outer border area with methylated spirits. Trace the pattern with a technical pen. Leave to dry for a few minutes.

8. Remove the pattern and place the panel on white paper. Using the colour guide (see page 151), paint the central spiral using a No. 4 paintbrush and yellow, orange and amber. Use the same colours to paint the three outer spirals. Apply the paints liberally straight from the bottle, allowing the colours to settle flat within the outlines. Leave to dry.

9. Paint all the green areas, then paint all the blue areas.

10. Mix green with clear paint and fill in all the light green areas.

11. Seal the interlaced border with light green. Apply the paint generously to seal the pen work.

12. Paint the three small circles and the outer border red. Leave to dry.

13. Glue a large glass droplet on to the central circle. Glue three smaller droplets into place using the dotted circles on the pattern as a guide. Leave to set.

14. Cut a 110cm (43¼in) length of 9mm (⅜in) lead with the scalpel. Press this round the edge of the panel so that 2mm (1/12in) is sticking to the glass with 7mm (¼in) hanging over the edge. Use the boning tool to rub the 2mm (1/12in) edge firmly on to the glass.

15. Position the panel on the window. Ask a friend to hold it in place while you press the overhanging lead on to the window. Rub the lead flat against the surface with the boning tool.

Window panel

As the sun shines through this vibrant spiral panel, your room will be bathed in colour.

Gilded bottle

A plain glass bottle is transformed into a Celtic treasure with some outliner and a few sheets of Dutch metal leaf. It is then aged with oil paint and embellished with gems.

Pattern for the gilded bottle.

Pattern for the Celtic vase opposite.

Opposite

Celtic vase

Self-adhesive lead is used to extend the decoration on this large vase. Keep the leaded lines simple to contrast with the complex painted spiral.

157

Patterns for the spiral designs opposite.

Spiral designs.

Knotwork Clip Frame

Learning to control the outliner is an essential part of glass painting. Try practising on paper until you can achieve a smooth even line, but remember that the lines do not have to be perfect – once painted, slight imperfections are less noticeable.

The paint should be applied liberally to achieve the truly flat finish required for this Celtic design. Once it is dry, a gem is added for that final flourish. Before you start, photocopy the design.

YOU WILL NEED

Clip frame, 20 x 25cm (8 x 10in)

White paper

Solvent-based glass paints: red, dark blue, turquoise, yellow, orange and green

Black outliner

No. 4 paintbrush

Cotton buds

Red glass droplet

Strong clear glue

Tip

For this project, you will need to place the outlined glass on top of a sheet of white paper while you are painting. Clip frames often have a sheet of paper inside which is white on the reverse and is ideal for this purpose.

Pattern for the knotwork clip frame. Enlarge on a photocopier by 170%.

1. Dismantle the clip frame and place the pattern under the glass. Reassemble the clip frame.

2. Use the tube of black outliner to carefully outline the central flower motif. Work around each flower petal and add the circular outer border. Leave the outliner to dry for half an hour.

3. Outline each corner Celtic knot. Turn the clip frame as you work, so that the knot is nearest you – this will prevent smudging. Leave the outliner to harden.

4. Dis... ...nd remove th... ...glass over a sheet ... the flower centr... then green, then tu... the inner petal section... middle sections turquoise... outer sections red.

5. Fill in the border around the flower in green.

6. Now paint each section between the green border. Begin by filling in with yellow. While the paint is still wet, add a line of orange around the edge. Use your paintbrush to gently pull the orange into the yellow until the paints merge and blend. Repeat until all the sections are filled in.

7. Use the same technique as shown in step 6 to paint in the corner Celtic knots. Create shading by blending orange where one area of knotwork crosses another.

8. Fill in the background areas using dark blue. Leave to dry. Fill in the remaining borders in red. Leave to dry.

9. Finally, glue a red glass droplet on to the centre of the flower. Leave to set.

162

Knotwork clip frame

The rich vibrant colours and strong black outlines found in Celtic designs are ideal for glass-painted projects. Celtic knots can be intricate and do demand good control of the outliner. Persevere – the results are well worth it!

Celtic mirror

This Celtic border design is enhanced by the use of imitation lead outliner, and by the simple addition of a glass droplet.

Pattern for the Celtic mirror opposite.

Paper Crafts

The first chapter of this book provides you with a myriad of Celtic design ideas – Celtic knots and spirals, zoomorphic designs depicting interlaced animals, intricate borders, and much more. This chapter shows you how to use Celtic designs to decorate paper craft items. Use foil to emboss a Celtic design for a Christmas card; transform a plain papier-mâché box into a Celtic treasure with a few paints and coloured crayons; create a funky Celtic frame and have fun with vibrant embellishments;

and, finally, decorate and age a book cover to encompass all your treasured poems and jottings.

All of the designs used in the projects in this chapter are provided here as templates that you can photocopy or trace. There are a number of books on the market which provide a rich source of Celtic designs and patterns, for example *Celtic Knotwork Designs* by Elaine Hill, *Celtic Borders and Motifs* by Lesley Davis and *The Complete Book of Celtic Designs*, all published by Search Press.

Celtic designs are both challenging and therapeutic in their intricacy and beauty. Enjoy this rich and fascinating journey.

Materials and Equipment

You will not need all of the items listed on these two pages for the projects. Each project provides you with a specific materials list for you to look at before you begin.

Basic materials

Pencil Use this to draw lines and to trace templates.

Eraser For removing pencil guide lines that are no longer needed.

Ruler Use a ruler to measure and draw straight lines, and with the back of a scalpel to score fold lines in card.

Scalpel Use this for cutting card. Use the back of the scalpel to score fold lines in card.

Compass For drawing circular designs accurately.

Cutting mat Cut card and paper with a scalpel on a cutting mat to prevent damage to your work surface.

Scissors Round-ended scissors are used for cutting paper and card. A pair of old scissors should be used for cutting embossing foil and wire.

Ballpoint pen Used for embossing foil.

Eyelet punch, **setter**, **hammer** and **mat** Use these for punching holes in card and for attaching eyelets.

Soft tissue Remove excess paint with a soft tissue when 'ageing' metal embellishments.

Spray adhesive Used to glue background paper on to card.

Strong clear adhesive Use this to glue embossing foil to card and to attach craft gems and embellishments.

Masking tape Secure patterns with masking tape before embossing.

Double-sided sticky pads Used to attach motifs to a base card to give a three-dimensional effect.

Flat paint brush This is used to paint frames and boxes before decorating them.

Sponge Use a small piece of sponge to apply acrylic paint.

Palette Used to hold small amounts of various paints.

Old pad of paper Use this as a padded surface when embossing foil.

Backing materials and blanks

A huge choice of backing papers, card and blanks is now available from art and craft shops. The selection shown here includes assorted coloured cards and papers, patterned background papers and embossing foils. Blank notebooks, sketchbooks and papier-mâché boxes are available in an assortment of sizes. Use thick card to create picture frames. The 'aged' label works well as a decoration on the Celtic book covers (see pages 190–191).

Paints, coloured pencils and inks

Acrylic paints and coloured inks are used to colour card and designs. Colour in detailed designs using coloured pencils. Age photocopied designs by staining them sepia using strong tea. Gold wax rubbed over a painted card surface and buffed with a soft tissue gives it a faded, aged look. Metallic outliners are ideal for adding detailed surface decoration by hand.

Embellishments

Ribbons, raffia, lettered fabric tape, gems, buttons, sequins, wire, eyelets, brads, skeleton leaves, shell, fabric and metal embellishments can all be used to decorate your Celtic projects.

A selection of papers, cards and blanks.

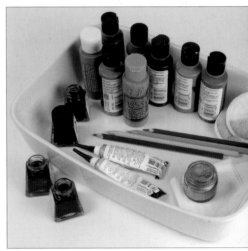

Materials you need to add colour to your Celtic designs.

Just some of the many embellishments you can use to decorate your paper craft projects.

169

Celtic Chimes

Celtic designs are perfect for metal-embossed work. This Christmas card uses a Celtic bell design to ring out its Christmas wish. With just a little embossing foil, some pretty paper and coloured card you can create a card to really impress your friends and family. It is inexpensive and good fun to do.

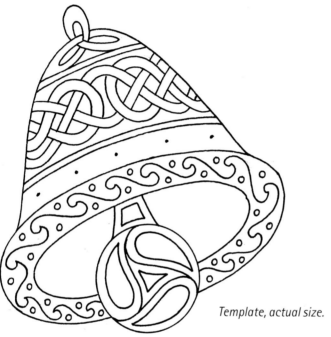

Template, actual size.

Template for the angel card variation (page 173), actual size.

1. Photocopy the pattern and tape it to the wrong side of the embossing foil.

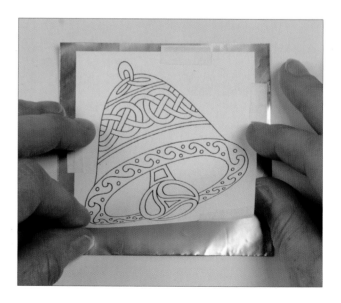

2. Resting your work on an old pad or folded newspaper, use a ballpoint pen to trace over the design, pressing firmly to achieve an embossed line on the foil. Turn the foil over to the front occasionally to check that you have traced the whole pattern.

3. Remove the pattern and trace over the design again to deepen the embossing.

4. Cut out the foil design using an old pair of scissors.

5. Cover the back of the design with strong glue.

6. Press the design on to a piece of white card and cut it out.

7. Place the design on a foam mat, and punch five holes, equally spaced across the bell.

8. Glue the floral paper square to the base card, and glue the red square on top.

9. Punch a hole at each corner of the red square.

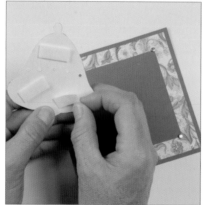

10. Attach a brad to each hole.

11. Apply double-sided sticky pads to the back of the embossed design.

12. Peel the backing off the pads and press the design on to the base card. Position it at a slight angle.

13. Attach a ribbon bow to the top of the bell using strong, clear glue.

The completed card is shown in the photograph opposite. The angel card was made using silver foil, with the angel worked within a typical Celtic arched window. She is backed with aged, patterned papers studded with metal brads and eyelets.

Decorated Box

Everybody needs a special box for their treasures and what better way to keep them safe than in this classic Celtic container. To achieve the classic look, the hexagonal box is first decorated with muted colours. A coloured pencil is used to shade the Celtic knot and finally buttons and ethnic sequins are used to create the 'studded' look.

Template, two-thirds actual size.

Templates for variations (page 178), two-thirds actual size.

YOU WILL NEED

Hexagonal papier-mâché box, approximately 5cm (2in) deep, 16cm (6¼in) across

Blue and black acrylic paints

Blue card

Blue coloured pencil

Eraser

Black felt-tip pen

Black buttons

Blue ethnic sequin embellishments

Large decorative button

Hole punch, hammer and mat

Paintbrush

Palette

Small piece of sponge

Compass

Spray glue and strong clear glue

Scalpel

Craft mat

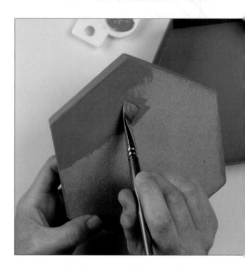

1. Paint the box and lid with blue acrylic paint.

2. When dry, sponge the edge of the lid with black paint.

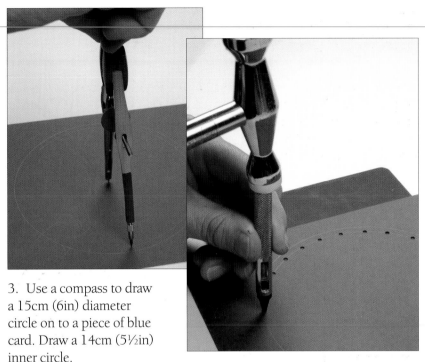

3. Use a compass to draw a 15cm (6in) diameter circle on to a piece of blue card. Draw a 14cm (5½in) inner circle.

4. Resting on a mat, punch holes around the inner circle. Remove the inner pencil line with an eraser.

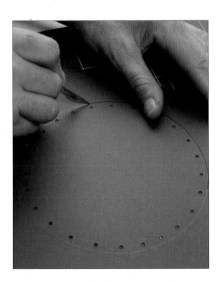

5. Cut around the outer circle using a scalpel and resting on a craft mat.

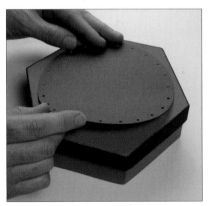

6. Glue the card circle to the box lid using spray glue.

7. Photocopy the design, enlarging it by fifty per cent, and shade the areas where the lines cross with a blue coloured pencil.

8. Colour the background areas with a black felt-tip pen.

9. Cut out the design and the central aperture, and glue the design to the box lid.

10. Glue a black button to each corner of the lid.

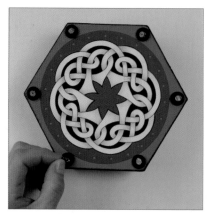

11. Top each button with a small blue sequin embellishment.

12. Glue a large button to the centre of the lid and decorate with a small blue embellishment.

The completed box.

Template for the serpent design on the pencil case shown opposite, two-thirds actual size.

The small square box above uses a coloured Celtic spiral motif as a central lid decoration, which is then embellished with gold brads. The design on the larger box is the same as that used in the project; the templates for the border and the spiral design on the smaller box are supplied on page 174.

This wooden pencil case is sponged with natural earthy colours to give it a textured, aged feel. When dry, the intertwining zoomorphic design is transferred on to the lid using transfer paper, then painted with muted colours to enhance the natural theme. Finally, the design is edged with a permanent felt-tip pen to give it definition.

Celtic Angel Frame

I am sure that if the Celtic artists had had 'shocking pink' in their colour palettes, they would definitely have used it. They loved vibrant colours. This card frame is painted with bright acrylic paints and inks and then embellished with metal charms, buttons, sequins, gems and metallic outliners. A real glitzy affair!

YOU WILL NEED

Thick card, two pieces, 8 x 14cm (3¼ x 5½in)

Acrylic paints, fuchsia and purple

Coloured inks, carmine, purple and sunshine yellow

Face and hand metal charms

Buttons, star sequins and assorted gems

Gold and silver outliners

Red wire

Palette and flat paintbrush

Spray glue and strong clear glue

Scalpel, cutting mat and ruler

Soft tissue

Templates for the frame, border and angel, actual size.

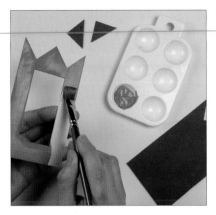

1. Cut the frame, the backing panel and two triangles from thick card using the template to help you.

2. Paint the backing panel and two triangles with purple acrylic paint and the frame with fuchsia.

3. When dry, glue the frame to the backing and the top triangle to the frame using strong clear adhesive.

4. Photocopy the templates for the angel and the border and randomly paint them with the coloured inks, overlapping the colours.

5. When dry, cut out the angel and the border and glue the figure so that it sits centrally within the aperture.

6. Glue the border to the bottom right-hand corner of the frame using spray adhesive, then attach the second triangle using strong glue.

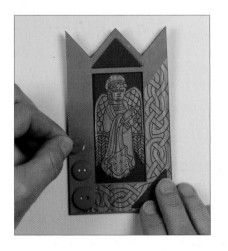

7. Glue three buttons down the left-hand side of the frame, with the largest at the bottom.

8. Glue three star sequins above the buttons and one to the lower triangle.

9. Decorate the frame with assorted gems.

10. Paint the metal hand and face charms with purple acrylic paint. Immediately wipe off the excess paint with a soft tissue.

11. When dry, glue the hand charm to the frame.

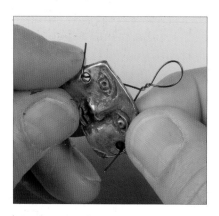

12. Loop and twist the middle of an 8cm (3¼in) length of wire. Thread the ends through the holes to the front of the face charm and bend the ends round to the back.

13. Glue the face to the top triangle using strong, clear glue.

14. Decorate the angel and the frame with gold and silver outliner.

The completed project.

Templates for the figures, torn border and triangular Celtic knot on the frame shown opposite , actual size.

This beard-tugging duo make the perfect central image for this funky frame. The basic frame is painted blue and decorated with buttons, sequins, gems, fleur-de-lys embellishments and metal charms. Dots and lines of metallic outliner are used to give the frame an encrusted, rich appearance.

Decorated Book Cover

Using simple techniques, this project allows you to create a book cover for a special diary or journal; the perfect gift for a close friend or relative. It suggests hidden treasures; secrets hidden by the mists of time. The paper on the cover has been aged using a wash of strong tea, and the addition of gold lettering, embossed metal foil and gold embellishments enhances the ancient feel of the book, and the suggestion of Celtic mysteries buried within its pages.

YOU WILL NEED

Notebook, approximately 11 x 15.5cm (4¼ x 6¼in)

Burgundy and black acrylic paint

3 teabags

Gold wax

Large vintage-style parcel label

Silver embossing foil

Spray glue and strong clear glue

Fabric heart embellishment

2 skeleton leaves

Gold paper wing embellishments

Red and gold lettered adhesive tape

Metal bell and key charms

Red cord, 1.25m (49¼in)

Ballpoint pen

Paintbrush

Old pad

Old scissors

Masking tape

Soft cloth or tissue

Large flat bowl

Templates for the border and bird design, actual size.

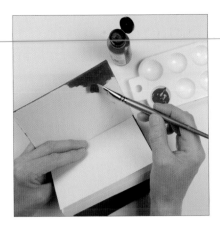
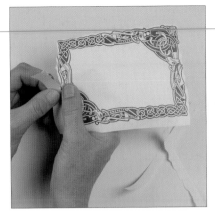

1. Paint the inside and outside cover of the book with burgundy acrylic paint and leave to dry.

2. Photocopy the border pattern twice and tear round the edges to give it a distressed look.

3. Make a strong black cup of tea using three teabags and pour it into a large flat bowl. Place your photocopies in the tea and leave for five or six hours, or overnight.

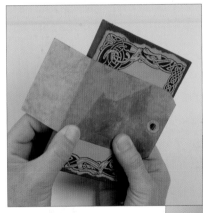

5. Bend the end 2cm (¾in) of the label upwards. Place the label on the front of the book and wrap it round the book to the back. Glue it in position.

4. Remove the photocopies and leave to dry. Glue one to the front of the book and one to the back using spray adhesive.

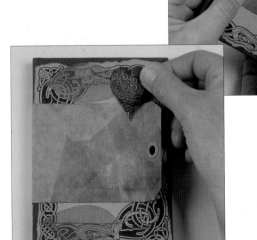

6. Glue the skeleton leaves and the heart embellishment on to the front cover.

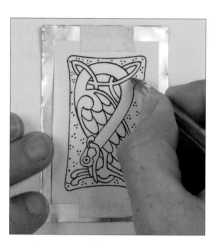

7. Run a line of lettered tape across the label and round to the back, and cut it off.

8. Photocopy the bird design and tape it to the back of the embossing foil. Trace over it with a ballpoint pen, pressing firmly. Work on an old paper pad.

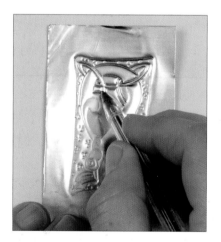

9. Remove the pattern and trace over the lines once more to deepen the embossing.

10. Cut out the bird design. Paint the side with the raised design and the two gold paper wings with burgundy and black acrylic paint.

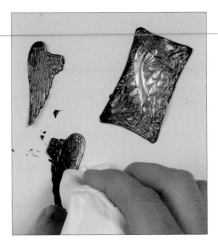

11. While the paint is still wet, remove the excess with a soft tissue to create an aged effect. Allow the paint to dry.

12. Glue the embossed bird to the label and a wing either side using clear, strong glue.

13. Rub over parts of the book cover and the spine with gold wax.

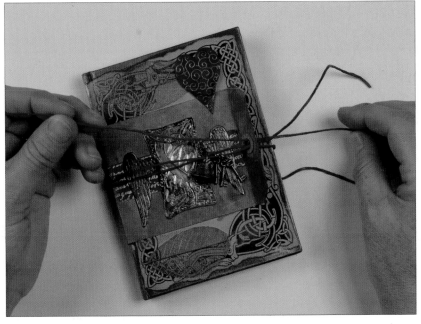

14. Buff the gold to a shine with a soft cloth or tissue.

15. Thread the bell and key charms on to a length of cord and wrap the cord around the book several times, each time threading it through the hole in the label. Tie the cord in a bow.

Left: This notebook cover is painted green and decoupaged with a tea-aged Celtic design and a vintage parcel label, as described in the project. The embossed image, skeleton leaves, metallic paper wings, cord, and small shell and mirror embellishments are used as decoration. The book is tied with green raffia thread embellished with bell charms.

Above and right: Templates for the dragon and face designs on the book cover shown above, half actual size.

Left: The completed project.

Index